REALITY TV:

HOW REAL IS REAL?

Institute of Ideas
Expanding the Boundaries of Public Debate

Dolan Cummings
Bernard Clark
Victoria Mapplebeck
Christopher Dunkley
Graham Barnfield

Hodder & Stoughton
A MEMBER OF THE HODDER HEADLINE GROUP

DEBATING MATTERS

791.45

Orders: please contact Bookpoint Ltd, 130 Milton Park, Abingdon, Oxon OX14
4SB. Telephone: (44) 01235 827720. Fax: (44) 01235 400454. Lines are
open from 9.00 - 6.00, Monday to Saturday, with a 24 hour message answering
service. You can also order through our website: www.madaboutbooks.com

British Library Cataloguing in Publication Data
A catalogue record for this title is available from
the British Library

ISBN 0 340 85735 8

First published 2002
Impression number   10 9 8 7 6 5 4 3 2
Year   2007 2006 2005 2004 2003

Typeset by Transet Limited, Coventry, England.
Printed in Great Britain for Hodder & Stoughton Educational, a division of
Hodder Headline Plc, 338 Euston Road, London NW1 3BH by Cox & Wyman,
Reading, Berks.

REALITY TV:

HOW REAL IS REAL?

Institute of Ideas
Expanding the Boundaries of Public Debate

DEBATING MATTERS

DEBATING MATTERS

CONTENTS

PREFACE
Claire Fox

NOTES ON THE CONTRIBUTORS

INTRODUCTION
Dolan Cummings

Essay One   **THE BOX OF TRICKS**
Bernard Clark

Essay Two   **MONEY SHOT**
Victoria Mapplebeck

Essay Three   **IT'S NOT NEW, AND IT'S NOT CLEVER**
Christopher Dunkley

Essay Four   **FROM DIRECT CINEMA TO CAR-WRECK VIDEO: REALITY TV AND THE CRISIS OF CONTENT**
Graham Barnfield

AFTERWORD
Dolan Cummings

 **PREFACE**

Since the summer of 2000, the Institute of Ideas (IOI) has organized a wide range of live debates, conferences and salons on issues of the day. The success of these events indicates a thirst for intelligent debate that goes beyond the headline or the sound-bite. The IOI was delighted to be approached by Hodder & Stoughton, with a proposal for a set of books modelled on this kind of debate. The *Debating Matters* series is the result and reflects the Institute's commitment to opening up discussions on issues which are often talked about in the public realm, but rarely interrogated outside academia, government committee or specialist milieu. Each book comprises a set of essays, which address one of four themes: law, science, society and the arts and media.

Our aim is to avoid approaching questions in too black and white a way. Instead, in each book, essayists will give voice to the various sides of the debate on contentious contemporary issues, in a readable style. Sometimes approaches will overlap, but from different perspectives and some contributors may not take a 'for or against' stance, but simply present the evidence dispassionately.

Debating Matters dwells on key issues that have emerged as concerns over the last few years, but which represent more than short-lived fads. For example, anxieties about the problem of 'designer babies', discussed in one book in this series, have risen over the past decade. But further scientific developments in reproductive technology, accompanied by a widespread cultural distrust of the implications of these developments, means the debate about 'designer babies' is set to continue. Similarly, preoccupations with the weather may hit the news at times of flooding or extreme weather conditions, but the underlying concern about global warming and the idea that man's intervention into nature is causing the world harm, addressed in another book in the *Debating Matters* series, is an enduring theme in contemporary culture.

At the heart of the series is the recognition that in today's culture, debate is too frequently sidelined. So-called political correctness has ruled out too many issues as inappropriate for debate. The oft noted 'dumbing down' of culture and education has taken its toll on intelligent and challenging public discussion. In the House of Commons, and in politics more generally, exchanges of views are downgraded in favour of consensus and arguments over matters of principle are a rarity. In our universities, current relativist orthodoxy celebrates all views as equal, as though there are no arguments to win. Whatever the cause, many in academia bemoan the loss of the vibrant contestation and robust refutation of ideas in seminars, lecture halls and research papers. Trends in the media have led to more 'reality TV', than TV debates about real issues and newspapers favour the personal column rather than the extended polemical essay. All these trends and more have had a chilling effect on debate.

But for society in general, and for individuals within it, the need for a robust intellectual approach to major issues of our day is essential. The *Debating Matters* series is one contribution to encouraging contest about ideas, so vital if we are to understand the world and play a part in shaping its future. You may not agree with all the essays in the *Debating Matters* series and you may not find all your questions answered or all your intellectual curiosity sated, but we hope you will find the essays stimulating, thought-provoking and a spur to carrying on the debate long after you have closed the book.

Claire Fox, Director, Institute of Ideas

NOTES ON THE CONTRIBUTORS

Graham Barnfield is a writer and former Senior Lecturer in Journalism at Surrey Institute of Art and Design University College. His PhD explored documentary and cultural policy in Roosevelt's New Deal. He is a former editor of *Culture Matters* (Sheffield Hallam University Press) and a contributor to various publications and audio-visual productions.

Bernard Clark has been broadcasting for 30 years, as a foreign correspondent, a news presenter, an executive producer, a documentary maker, and an independent producer. He originated the BBC's *Watchdog* and *Bookmark*, and Channel 4's *Hard News*. In the early 1980s he started Clark TV which has made series and documentaries for all the major British broadcasters, and many abroad, especially the US and Japan.

Dolan Cummings works at the Institute of Ideas, and is commissioning editor for the Arts and Media section of the *Debating Matters* series. He is the author of *In Search of Sesame Street: Policing Civility for the 21st Century* (Sheffield Hallam University Press, 1999) and he writes a weekly television column for www.spiked-online.com.

Christopher Dunkley is a journalist and broadcaster and was television critic for the *Financial Times* between 1973 and 2002. He began his journalistic career at the *Slough Observer* in 1963 and has also worked for the *UK Press Gazette* and *The Times*, and written widely on broadcasting issues. He presented BBC Radio Four's *Feedback* programme between 1986 and 1998.

Victoria Mapplebeck is a writer and filmmaker in the UK. She writes media criticism for *The Guardian* and *The Observer*. Her films include *Meet the Kilshaws*, an intimate documentary portrait of fast-track celebrities, Alan and Judith Kilshaw. She also conceived and directed *Smart Hearts*, Channel Four's first documentary/web convergence project. *Smart Hearts*, an online and series portrait of a contemporary marriage, was nominated for a 2001 New Media Indie Award. *Smart Hearts* is regularly selected for think tanks and film festivals developing innovative approaches to documentary and new media.

INTRODUCTION
Dolan Cummings

Reality TV is a strange idea. The implication is that other TV is somehow unreal. On one level this is obviously true: even leaving aside explicitly fictional drama, TV mainly comprises extremely artificial formats: gameshows, studio-based news programmes, sitcoms and so on. Even documentaries tend to follow quite misleading conventions; for example, presenters often begin by pretending not to know what they are about to tell us. The question then is whether Reality TV really is an exception to this rule, or whether it employs unreal conventions of its own.

So what is Reality TV? Examples include everything from ITV's *Survivor*, in which participants must survive on a desert island or other remote location, to E4's *Chained*, in which young singles are chained to members of the opposite sex. Docusoaps such as the BBC's *Driving School* and talent contests like ITV's *Popstars* are also sometimes included in discussions about Reality TV. How have these different programmes all come to be thought of as part of the same genre? What they have in common, as the contributors in this book discuss, is a preference for 'ordinary people'.

As Bernard Clark explains in his essay, however, Reality TV has a long and interesting prehistory. Long before *Big Brother*, documentary makers endeavoured to put 'real people' on television, and to let them tell their own stories. What is now discussed as Reality TV, though, is something quite different. Reality TV is now generally understood to mean programmes that feature members of the public in unusual situations, often competing for a prize, and often involving audience participation. Producers sometimes claim that the programmes have value as documentary or even anthropology, but the 'Reality TV' label is generally reserved for entertainment programmes. The Reality TV 'ethic', however, has influenced factual programming more broadly. History programmes, for example, increasingly take the form of reconstructions, with members of the public living in iron age or World War One conditions. Everybody who works in television knows that programme ideas with a 'reality' component are more likely to be commissioned than more conventional ones.

Reality TV's archetype, of course, is *Big Brother*, which features a group of contestants in a specially designed house fitted with cameras which monitor the 'housemates' 24 hours a day. The contestants are given tasks to perform in return for extra food and other treats, and to encourage them to interact in various ways and get to know one another. Every week, they each nominate their least favourite housemate, the two contestants with the most nominations are announced and the public are invited to vote one of them out of the house. In this way the contestants are gradually whittled away, and whoever is left in the house at the end of the series is the winner and gets a cash prize.

Part of the appeal of *Big Brother* is that it involves 'real people', plucked from obscurity and turned into stars, not because of any special talent, but just because they seem personable. *Big Brother* is literally a personality contest. More than that, the contestants' fate is in the hands of more 'ordinary people', the audience itself. For this reason, *Big Brother* has even been described as democratic. It has also been pointed out that while participation in parliamentary elections seems to be in terminal decline, thousands of people take part in the *Big Brother* telephone polls. Perhaps then, argue some, the goings on in the *Big Brother* house are more 'real' for ordinary people than the goings on at Westminster.

Critics of Reality TV see this kind of rhetoric as part of the problem. Reality TV has featured strongly in the discussion about 'dumbing down', which emerged in the mid-1990s. It is contended that our culture has become vulgar and unintelligent, and that television, along with the rest of the media, now caters to 'the lowest common denominator' (sex, celebrity and voyeuristic sensationalism), rather than challenging the audience. From this point of view, the 'ordinariness' of the *Big Brother* contestants is nothing to be celebrated. The idea of 'democratizing' television, certainly if that means downgrading talent and abandoning standards, is anathema to anyone who believes in the 'Reithian' ideal. (Lord Reith was the founding father of the BBC, and is associated with the idea that broadcasters ought to aim just above the level of the average viewer, in order to improve the audience.) Rather than simply 'giving the people what they want', the Reithian ideal is to give them something better, in the belief that they will learn to appreciate it.

This kind of thinking has fallen foul of the anti-elitism that, for better or worse, pervades contemporary culture. The idea that anyone in authority (or indeed anyone at all) should decide what is 'better' has become something of a taboo. At a seminar organized by the British Academy of Film and Television Arts (BAFTA), Gary Carter of the entertainment company Endemol, and a key figure in the distribution of *Big Brother*, gave a speech on the future of Reality TV (25 February 2002). Carter explained how the public attitude to television has changed over the last two generations, from accepting the medium as an unquestioned source of authority, to a more critical and savvy engagement. When television was new, people tended to think of it as a reflection of objective reality. A BBC presenter was not simply a man on television, but 'the man on television'. The next generation, people now in their forties, grew up at a time when television had a history, and was understood as part of culture rather than a simple reflection of reality. There was even television about television, and people began to think more critically about the medium.

Today, the man on television is just another voice amid the hubbub of a high-tech multimedia age. Young people in particular have little or no automatic respect for the medium itself; they take it for granted that documentaries are subjective, and even news and current affairs programmes will be biased in one way or another. This reflects a broader shift in the way that we understand reality. It is not simply that people are more sophisticated now, and therefore less inclined to believe everything they see on TV, though that may well be true. Today it is no longer taken for granted that there even is such a thing as objective reality.

In the absence of an agreed frame of reference in the real world, broadcasters simply cannot command the kind of authority they once did, and programme makers must look for other ways to engage or connect with their audiences. This has become a major concern at the BBC: indeed Lord Reith's famous remit for the corporation, 'to entertain, inform and educate' has now been updated to include 'connect'. For Gary Carter, the solution is to give viewers greater control over what they watch. This is where the 'democratic' aspect of Reality TV comes into its own. Giving people the opportunity to interact directly with television programmes fundamentally transforms the way they relate to the medium. Viewers can even use the internet and mobile phones to keep up with what is happening and have their say. Rather than simply accepting what broadcasters choose to dish out, how and when broadcasters see fit, young people can fit the medium into their own lifestyles, and expect it to reflect their own concerns.

Clearly, if all this is true then the rise of Reality TV is just one aspect of a broader shift in public life and social mores. By looking in depth at this particular phenomenon, the four essays that follow tell us a great deal about these changes in society at large as well as current trends in the TV schedules.

Bernard Clark looks at the history of documentary, drawing on his own experience of making programmes about 'ordinary people' in the 1970s. For Clark, the idea that TV programmes could somehow be 'real' was always tenuous; producers and editors inevitably distort reality, both intentionally and unintentionally. Clark feels that his own early work did achieve a limited but refreshing level of realism. As the subjects of documentaries became more and more savvy, however, and especially once TV turned its attention to the image-conscious middle classes, the pretence of realism became totally unsustainable. Since documentary has exhausted itself, what passes for reality now is something very different. Clark regards Reality TV as a contradiction in terms and argues that the more producers claim to be dealing with reality, the less true this is likely to be.

Victoria Mapplebeck picks up where Clark leaves off. She is sceptical of traditional documentary's claim to objectivity, and offers instead a newer model of documentary-making. Rather than pretending to present the unmediated truth, producers ought to let their subjects speak for themselves, and let the viewers come to their own conclusions. For example, Mapplebeck discusses the potential of webcams, small cameras that can be used to observe people 24 hours a day, with the footage available directly on the internet. Having used webcams in her own programme *Smart Hearts*, Mapplebeck is aware of the trade-off between editorial control and access, but she feels it is sometimes worth sacrificing a little of the former for more of the latter. Mapplebeck argues that this approach also counters the allegation that Reality TV is a form of voyeurism. As long as the subject gives his or her consent, the charge of voyeurism is little more than a snobbish cliché.

Reality TV is criticized in the next essay, by Christopher Dunkley, on two counts. First he argues that it is not nearly as new as it is often claimed. The idea of filming people isolated on a remote island, for example, goes back as far as the 1950s. More importantly, Dunkley argues that what is now called Reality TV emerged not from the documentary genre at all, but from game shows. Something like *Big Brother* has far more in common with the wacky *It's a Knockout!* than with a documentary such as Paul Watson's *The Family*, he contends. The producer's concern is less with documenting the real world than with entertaining large audiences. Dunkley's second objection is that the entertainment derived from Reality TV is increasingly at the expense of the participants. On a trivial level, people are often encouraged to make fools of themselves for the cameras. More seriously, Reality TV thrives on emotional exposure. Whereas Victoria Mapplebeck argues that this can be a valuable component of serious documentary, Dunkley suggests that it is humiliation for sheer entertainment value.

The bulk of Graham Barnfield's essay is concerned with the documentary tradition. Like Dunkley, he wants to make a distinction between documentary and entertainment, but Barnfield sees the recent history of documentary as an important influence on Reality TV. He looks at how two schools of documentary-making, direct cinema and ciné-verité, expressed prevailing attitudes to authority and realism in the 1960s. Both acknowledged the difficulty of achieving objectivity, while striving in different ways to get as close to the truth as possible. For Barnfield, what is important is that there was a debate about the best way to do this. Film-makers' preoccupation with technical aspects of documentary expressed an underlying commitment to the content. Barnfield argues that the rise of Reality TV reflects a loss of faith in objective truth. Whereas in the past, 'the truth' was fiercely debated, paradoxically today's relativistic climate means that the 'reality' label is accepted uncritically.

In the spirit of critical thinking, then, it is worth asking whether there really is such a thing as Reality TV at all. Some argue that Reality TV is just a passing fad in light entertainment and should not be taken seriously. But assuming that Reality TV is here to stay, is it simply a new genre with a distinctive set of conventions, or does it reflect a broader transformation of television as a medium? This book sets outs the argument, and we hope it will provoke readers to think critically and imaginatively about the strange world of Reality TV.

Essay One

THE BOX OF TRICKS
Bernard Clark

A few years ago, I investigated the industrial production of food. It seems that ice-cream is made of pig fat; the flavour in coffee granules is artificially sprayed on after roasting; chemical fragrance is added to whisky; and meat has more dye than the average sweater. My investigation showed that very little of our food was 'real', and that the message on the packaging was generally in inverse proportion to its artificiality; that is, if the food was highly manufactured, the packaging suggested it was particularly authentic, probably traditionally so.

You might think this is a strange way to begin an essay on 'Reality TV', but to me the parallels are obvious. Whether it is called 'observational documentary', 'fly-on-the-wall', 'real-life-soap', or whatever, a lot of 'Reality TV' is now no more authentic than a take-away hamburger meal and even less nutritious. And the less authentic the production, the more the presentation will bang on about 'unprecedented access' and feign 'reality'.

THE ORIGINS OF REALITY TV

This homogenization occurred in factual television, as with manufactured food, because of customer demand; television is an industry after all. If people want to eat bits of carcass disguised as meat, someone, somewhere, will provide; ditto television. So documentary producers have provided the public with programmes that are disguised entertainment – amateur actors pretending to fall in and out of love, old women pretending to learn to drive, or families seeming to live like their great grandparents. While TV has exposed the artificiality in other marketplaces, it has yet to turn the zoom lens on itself, perhaps because 'Reality TV' is a new phenomenon, indeed a new concept. Until 30 years ago no one suggested that documentary was 'real' in the recent sense of the word. The equipment was too heavy, the film too expensive, so everything was staged for the camera.

For instance, with Richard Cawston's 1969 documentary for the BBC *The Royal Family*, no one pretended that this would reveal a natural, real-life portrait of the Queen, just that we would glimpse a few more informal 'set-ups' than previously. I remember being a little shocked to see the Queen driving a car and chatting to her obsequious lackies – indeed talking at all – but the overall effect was of an ordinary woman with banal attitudes living an extraordinary life, which in itself was revelatory. But the entire programme was, in fact, staged – even the royal Corgis appear to be playing to the camera – and neither the producer nor the royal personages pretended otherwise. Three decades ago this was typical documentary – class-conscious, polite, unobtrusive and modest – an art-form that knew its place.

However, while Cawston was putting the finishing touches on *The Royal Family*, just along the corridor at the BBC's Kensington House, another part of his unit was working on a revolution. Paul Watson was developing a wholly new concept that would change the nature of factual television, ironically also called *The Family*, albeit about the lowly Wilkins family in Reading. That juxtaposition, between the honestly mannered, stiff documentaries of the old-school-tie and the in-yer-face, soap-style show about ordinary working folk, was the foundation of 'Reality TV', although at the time, the early 1970s, none of us called it that. The ideas were too arbitrary for such an elevated description. To us it was just an experimental process of gut-instinct filming, followed by showing what seemed vaguely interesting and could be justified to the bosses.

In 1973, John Slater at Granada in Manchester said to me, 'A good director can make a film about nothing – anywhere, any time, with no research and no story.' We were on a long train journey and, as the wine flowed, a faraway look came into in his eyes. 'Throw a dart into an A–Z town map. Wherever it lands you go with a film-crew and make a film about that street. It will be terrific.' Slater was my boss, and distinctly mad, so I shuddered and avoided him for several weeks; but every time we passed in the corridor he would return to the same mantra. 'A street, Bernard, go and film a street, any street. Do it.' So finally, with a sinking heart, I chose the nearest Clark Street to the Granada studios in Salford and set off one morning, with cameraman Mike Blakely, to make a film at random. Clark Street was the typical Coronation Street, a hundred yards long, several dozen two-up-two-downs on both sides, outside toilets and scrubbed doorsteps. We stood there. Mike asked, 'What's the story?' I shrugged, 'There isn't one.' The sound-recordist muttered, 'Let's pray for an air crash.' But, nothing happened. Nothing at all. Except it began to rain. 'I'll shoot some moodies,' Mike said helpfully.

Then a front door opened and an elderly lady waddled over with a tray and three cups. 'You the man off telly?' she asked. 'What are you doing here?' I still remember her name. It was Mrs Langridge. 'Oooh, I can tell yer some stories, love, as happened here in street!' Mike switched his camera on. 'Girl at number eight, it isn't his son, husband thinks it is, but oh no. And them at 19, now I mind me own business, live and let live, but ...' While Mike continued filming, with the microphone pointing straight into her face, Mrs Langridge looked both ways to check she wasn't being overheard and said, 'Keep this under your hat, dear, but she's been inside, electric meter, I mean she's nice enough in her way.' That was the beginning of Clark Street and, for me, the beginning of 'Reality TV'.

Each week I picked a street at random, and the residents were the content and the stars, just talking about their lives and the neighbours – a series that ran to 58 editions. The show was immediately very popular and none of us understood why. One executive thought he did: 'Because nothing much happens, like their lives,' he opined, 'and because the films are real.' In my view he was wrong on both counts.

 NEVER A DULL MOMENT

A hundred and sixty people lived in that street in Salford, about 30 families and 40 pensioners. Statistically the street might expect 2.4 deaths per year, a similar number of births, a little under two marriages, and one divorce. Five houses would change hands with all the disruption and attendant intrigue of new neighbours, a handful of cats would go missing, and several dogs die. That's just for starters, before we begin on the domestic violence, the serious illnesses, the love-triangles and the weirdo at number 36 who ran off with a schoolgirl. Who says nothing happens in a street of 54 ordinary houses? As Mrs Langridge said, 'It's all go, dear, never a dull. Like Evette in 23, won £19,000 on the pools. Went on a cruise and met whats-her-name. We call them 'the girl-friends', they're OK – nice.'

Is that a story? You bet it is. For our street-level audience, it is as ordinary, special and compulsive as soap opera, and this is why the programmes were so popular. Close-up candid and frank, what we filmed was real – real-life. When Mrs Langridge said, 'Keep this under your hat' and ignored our microphone, it was because she could not relate the film-crew and myself to the telly she watched every night. To her, we were just a trio of scruffy men in her street with a couple of bits of equipment. True, she recognized me as a reporter, but that did not mean she could really connect me with her television, or ever conceive that she would actually appear herself, on that box of tricks in the corner of her lounge. In her mind, television was far too important to just turn up one day in her ordinary street. Even though we told her, she still could not really believe it and nor could many of the thousands of people I eventually spoke to. In their hearts they believed I was an ordinary bloke asking ordinary questions which they answered with the earthy honesty as if we were in the pub. After a day of shooting on Clark Street the question became – what to leave out? Which is when the manipulation started and is the reason the films were not real.

◆ ● ●
● ● ●
● ● ◆ **THE DECEPTION**

On an average Clark Street, I would shoot about five times more material than I would use – a very efficient ratio by today's standards. So four-fifths of the filmed truth would be thrown away, as decided by me. And that process of selection back at base had one overwhelming function, to package the maximum amount of entertainment and cor-blimey interest into the unforgiving on-air minute. This did not, of necessity, make the programme un-real; just that all editing is a compromise against available airtime and reality was not a significant factor. I was far more important. Yes, ME. The ego of the film-maker, the post-production wizard with people's lives in his hands. Let me give you a for-instance. In one of the films, on a street in Rochdale, a pugnacious young mother was saying much of nothing when she suddenly froze. 'Oh, I've left a pan on the stove,' she said, and dashed off into her house. The camera continued to turn for about half a minute, on a monotonous, empty front door. Then she came back wiped her hands, looked at the camera and said, 'Now where was I?' CUT.

This was, of course, delightful, and way ahead of its time. Directors did not fill TV screens with emptiness in the early 1970s, then ruthlessly cut. Colleagues slapped me on the back, said, 'Gee, that was real', called me a star, and I lapped it up. The edit-suite god had come up trumps.

So what had actually occurred? A woman had taken her pan off the stove in the middle of a conversation. Big deal. But it seemed so real because it had happened on the telly, which until then had left such incidental nothings on the cutting-room floor. It is only the fact of it being on television that gives such an inane event any validity at all, a major key to all 'reality' output. I knew this, and ruthlessly used its very ordinary monotony as part of my entertainment pitch. Real? Do me a favour. Reality would have been listening to what the lady said after she came back, but I wanted the audience to have a laugh.

Does this surprise you? Well, it shouldn't. That's television, and I am happy to admit it. Clark Street was more 'real' than any programme I have seen since, but the overall experience has made me wary of anyone who talks of 'Reality TV'. The two words are mutually exclusive at the most basic level. Television is merely a collection of lines across a screen collected from a camera and microphone, then reassembled through a series of electronic devices. You might think that is obvious but the whole industry, the art and the craft, conspires to pretend otherwise until the producers and the audience forget it's just organized electricity. And if the whole caboodle is false, how can any part of it be real? Answer: it can't. There is no such thing as 'real TV', just different degrees of 'un-realness'. At one level that does not matter. We don't believe the newsreader is really sitting in the box in the corner of our lounge – that's absurd. But we do believe that he's speaking to us personally, because it feels like he is – that's the effect a newsreader tries to create. And yet he's in an antiseptic studio talking to glass encased in metal and plastic, smiling at the lens, looking down occasionally, naturally, as if he were our trusted friend. If you stop to think about it, that's absurd too. A grown man being paid a couple of hundred thousand a year to talk earnestly to a piece of glass and plastic. UN-real.

Furthermore, he isn't even talking to a lens; he's reading the words off a teleprompt. What? So he's not in the box in the corner of my room chatting to me, he's reading someone else's script? Of course you knew that anyway, and we're happy to go along with it, because it's how news programmes work, we all know it's false, don't we? Well, yes and no. I know because I read the news for a few years and very boring it was too. But the audience do not give it a moment's thought, they just react personally to the image they are seeing and, at that personal level, they suspend disbelief. A good newsreader becomes, in the viewers' psyche, part of their extended family, and therefore psychically real.

Over the years there have been several experiments to replace the human newsreader with a robot; none has worked, presumably because the human element is missing. It seems we need the illusion of a person talking to us to feel comfortable, even though at a deeper level we know it's digital confetti. This paradox – the unconscious versus the conscious – is at the heart of the recent debate on Reality TV. Until a few decades ago, the subject did not arise; we all knew television was artificial. It had to be. The equipment was so heavy, the lights were so bright and celluloid so expensive there was no point trying to convince the audience they were witnessing reality. In *The Family*, about the Wilkins family of Reading in the early 1970s, there was no such pretence; Paul Watson went out of his way to include the crew and the production team and, indeed, towards the end of the series television itself became part of the story. It seemed real because, until then, television had been formal, set up, seemingly a preordained dance between subject, producer and audience. Watson changed that because he stayed back, filmed only what the Wilkins family naturally did, without coaching or suggestion from the director. I use the word 'naturally' with some hesitation, as Watson would himself, because no member of a family, not even the brazen Mrs Wilkins, acts entirely naturally while being filmed. At best the camera is a catalyst, at worst the main purpose, for actions and argument which probably wouldn't happen in that form if the camera were not present.

As the series meandered towards its climax, Watson's particular genius was to demonstrate this by showing the first eight or so programmes while still filming the last few, so that television itself became part of the plot – the final programmes incorporated the media furore that built up over the series, creating a cross-pollination, like a hall of mirrors, that has never been equalled. Television creates fuss, then films the consequences of that fuss, which in turn causes more fuss. Little wonder that *The Family* flew off the documentary audience scale. Astonishingly, very few producers copied *The Family*, perhaps because it did at that time seem to be a definitive work.

True, Roger Graef was producing *The Space Between Words*, a rather more serious attempt to film 'reality' in the workplace, which did not entirely succeed, probably because of the self-consciousness of the white-collar subjects. Graef later followed this up with his acclaimed series *The Police*, again in Reading, but the journalistic strength of the programmes, especially those on rape, were such that the remarkable

observational aspects received less notice. Graef was an uncom-
promising artist, more rigorous in the edit-suite than Watson; along
with his fanatically non-interventionist cameraman Charles Stewart,
he got closer to true reality than anyone in the next 25 years.

A MATTER OF CLASS

It is also interesting that both *The Family* and *The Police* were filmed
in Reading. Partly, I fear, it was to do with proximity to the BBC
studios in west London, but another reason, perhaps unwitting, had to
do with class. Back then, in the 70s, market researchers would head
for Reading to test new products. The city was known to be a
microcosm of the population of Britain: if the people of Reading liked
the flavour of a particular frozen pea, so would the nation. Reading
had a very healthy working class, certainly for a city in the south east,
and it was the working class that would be most natural on camera –
essentially less stuffy than the mannered middle-classes.

This sense that the working classes would reveal all on television was well
known to documentary makers then, indeed it became a feature of Clark
Street. The Director of Programmes at Granada, David Plowright, summed
it up succinctly. 'You are making programmes in which the working class
are showing themselves up, albeit endearingly, so the middle-classes can
have a chuckle.' That was true, as it is of *Coronation Street*. This did not
mean the working class were cynically used by educated programme
makers but it's worth noting that the reality genre cut its teeth among
subjects who did not fully appreciate what was happening when the
filming began. In a phrase they were 'camera fodder', and happy to be
so, but inevitably, as time passed, the practitioners of reality turned their
lenses towards more elusive and 'elevated' individuals, the less trusting,
less dupable, but blossoming middle-classes.

In particular, Peter Moore at Channel 4's Cutting Edge built a solid reputation on the back of one-off documentaries on middle-class home-owners' subjects, some of which I produced. *Housing Chain*, *Family Feuds* and *Trouble with the Neighbours* were programmes of their Thatcherite times, hitting the audience jackpot, and later being stripped into series by BBC1 or ITV. The usual sub-text was money, not in the old poverty sense, but in the 'grab-what-you-can' supermarket ethos of independent citizens. Britain was changing before the television watchers' eyes, as jobs-for-life became a distant memory and the mines closed forever. I will always remember filming the ultimate reality during the 1987 election, from a middle-aged miner, sitting on his new three piece suite, in his owned house near Doncaster, his and hers cars in the garage outside. 'Damn that Thatcher woman,' he muttered. 'She's taken our lives away, but made us rich. Damn her.'

However, there were bastions still to crack. The most enthralling, and by far the most honest, series went beyond the middle classes; it embroiled the upper class in all its glory. In the mid-90s, *The House* told the story of the Royal Opera House in full-blown crisis – screaming fits, walk-outs, warts and all. A real-life docusoap opera. Unfairly described as Jeremy Isaac's suicide note, I watched all the gorgeous fun enthralled, grateful that such sophisticated media operatives did not know better. But presumably the be-Knighted backroom boys and girls couldn't resist being household names for a while, however much the Pall Mall club-land culture-vultures tut-tutted.

Therein lies a snobbish British truth – that it is unseemly for our established elite to let it all hang out before the television masses or, indeed, to reveal anything whatsoever. *The House* was produced for the BBC, so I tried a subversive trick of my own and approached the BBC to propose a 'fly-on-the-wall' observational reality series about the BBC itself. After all, if they refused, while continuing to approach all and sundry to open up their doors, it would be rank hypocrisy. The BBC did not give it a moment's thought. 'Of course not,' they replied with just a hint of outrage in their voice, 'Who do you take us for?'

We can now look back and see that *The House* was the end of innocence for 'reality' television, a watershed had been reached. The traditional working class were thinning out and in any case had lost their folksy allure, the middle-class had been done to death and our institutions were suspicious as hell. Our rulers, or at least a small but symbolic clique of them, had been caught and the Establishment was onto the case. Henceforth, access would be guarded and pinned down by lawyers, and overseen by corporate politicians. Permissions became grudging and cautious, audiences harder to find; the easy talent began to move on. 'Reality' at least in the documentary sense, wasn't worth the bother.

THE NEW REALITY

I first understood this one Tuesday in July 1996 on a mobile at my son's cricket match. An excellent Channel 4 lawyer, the kind who wants to help get programmes on the air, was patiently explaining the number of permissions we would require for a series about love and hate at work. I said, 'It would be easier to hire an old army camp, sign up a few dozen volunteers and pay them to pretend.' He replied, very quickly, 'Yes, it would.' I went back to the cricket, little realizing we had almost invented *Big Brother*.

A process was now underway, a move from perceived 'reality' to blatant, no-holds-barred artifice. The serious observational documentary would be downgraded to support billing, while specially recruited 'ordinary' people would become the stars. After all, this did not seem such a new departure because producers had been manipulating the shot footage in the edit suite since the early days of documentary; but now they started manipulating the filming, and sometimes the 'cast-list' before filming even began. The 'ordinary' people they chose conspired with producers to play roles and 'act-up the part' in varying degrees of falsehood.

At this point, the latish 1990s, the reality story forks down two very different roads: One, the unashamed, relatively straightforward entertainment shows such as *Big Brother* and *Castaway Island* (more later). Two, the docusoap series and hybrid 'pretend' documentaries like *Daddy's Girl* and *Builders*. I was enthralled by *Builders* – a show that seemed to have everything. The complaining sequence, several minutes on virtually a single shot, was one of the finest pieces of documentary I shall ever see, full of movement, mood and character. The only problem – it wasn't documentary. The complainer was acting a part; therefore it was drama, which in that context means it was a lie. When I first discovered that, I nearly cried – because I was duped, I had believed, I had been enthralled. My feeling in retrospect is that *Builders* signalled the end of observational, reality documentary.

The clue lay not in that sequence, or in the hapless producer, or the even more hapless commissioning editor who let it pass into broadcast legend; the clue lay in the desperation that had made it likely to happen. Observational documentary had lost confidence in itself to be a plain and honest story well told. Why? There are several schools of thought. One, as stated above, is that because of the past success of the genre and the rise of the docu-soaps, the obvious subjects had been exhausted, the audience had seen it all and needed increasing sensation to tune in. Another, is that the commissioning system had become fiercely competitive, with fewer spaces reserved for 'quality' observational documentary, mirrored elsewhere in the way soap-opera had chased out quality drama. However, in my view, the primary reason lay in a 'moral collapse', primarily inside the broadcasters, but followed, perhaps necessarily, by the documentary programme-makers.

Broadcasters control all the airtime and have all the money; programme-makers have to stay in step in order to make films and eat. It is not a chicken and egg, the broadcasters are both, and they frequently cited 'competition' as a kind of tyranny to pressurize the producers to cut corners and sensationalize. But when the documentary ethos collapsed, and the press unravelled several programmes as fakes, the broadcasters feigned amazement, then washed their hands and turned to their lawyers to blame producers. Perhaps producers should have been less pliant, but broadcasters should not have demanded sensation in the first place. By then, the late 1990s, I had mainly stepped back, so I watched the incriminations and counter-incriminations from the sidelines. In any case, the reality circus had moved onto the docu-soaps and factual entertainment.

Ironically, it was the collapse of traditional entertainment, especially situation comedy on BBC1, which led to the explosion of docusoaps and the subsequent inventing of the reality game shows. Not only were docusoaps such as *Airport* and *Driving School* reliably popular, but compared with sitcoms they were cheap, too. Such formats only required malleable but forthright characters who could act naturally while keeping half an eye on the camera. Ideally, they would also combine caricature with human vulnerability and be, oh, you know, suggestible, without actually being told how to act by the director. Well, maybe a bit more than suggestible – maybe the subjects could 'do it like this?' as some directors hinted in private, when the camera was in its box.

These hybrids, the mass-market, everyday docusoaps masquerading as 'slices of real life', turned out to be the most dishonest of all the factual output, not because they were staged, but because they pretended not to be. It is not 'reality' if an incident occurs on the fourth take or at the behest of the director, but these shows are not honestly packaged like a Big Mac, but are packaged up like organic produce. But do we care? Certainly the audience doesn't – it cares less about what goes into a television programme than what goes into its food. I can become pompous about the more nutritious fare that's being squeezed out of the documentary mix these days, but it's pointless to whinge. Ultimately, the people want what they want – reality with an aaahhh – sod the deeper truths. Or any truth at all.

In any case, the docusoaps have in turn been upstaged by the reality game shows, such as *Big Brother*, *Survival* and *Popstars*, as entertainment with a capital E fights back. Refreshingly, neither the participants nor the producers make any claims about reality or truth, other than in the context of a devious contest to win cash, always a good honest way to reveal the real nature of people. As the label clearly shows, these programmes are staged and artificial, with stagy and artificial characters, and proud of it. I call it 'rentertainment' (as in 'renting' the lives of the participants for fun – and ratings). And it's within the game show genre that 'reality' on television will evolve most in the future. Entertainment producers will continue to plunder the factual area as they search for yet more compulsive formats that will bring us closer and closer to that Hollywood classic, the *Truman Show*.

I foresee entire lives being played out in front of the cameras, with the home audience making turning-point decisions such as should a character take a job, should a couple have a baby, or should a pensioner agree to a risky operation? If the audience has helped to decide, it will be more involved in the consequences and therefore more likely to watch. For instance, 'Should Rita marry Ricky? Vote NOW.' If you don't believe this is imminent, that one has already happened. But we are actually just winching up the roller-coaster before the journey begins; over the next decade or so we are in for an enthralling ride.

Imagine, for a moment, a combination of *Seven Up* (Mike Apted's massively important every-seven-years documentary series for Granada) and *Popstars*. But now the audience is in the delivery room to watch lives begin, and can vote for which babies get prizes or nothing. We see the effect and revisit – some kids win private education, designer clothes etc. The possibilities are endless and will be thoroughly exploited. These 'reality' game shows will eclipse the *Truman Show* in one crucial way; the home audience will be continually intervening, indeed controlling, the hapless lives they are watching. I suspect it will not be too long before a murder occurs, directly related to the competitive culture these shows represent or, more accurately, the culture of humiliation. After all, the audience fascination is not just for watching 'their' life-participant win; it's for watching how the others react when they lose. I foresee lots of work for high-priced lawyers, but the producers will be able to afford it. Through limited companies, they will have squeezed many fortunes from their rentertainment participants and leave others to clear up the real human mess left behind.

CONCLUSION

In that context what chance traditional documentary? None. It will become an art form and, therefore, a vanity 'hobby' kept alive by the subsidy of low-maintenance producers and rich patricians. Perhaps surprisingly, that does not worry me – forms of expression move on, though I am a trifle sad. Documentary did enliven the mix – an exquisite, often indulgent, seasoning will now gather dust at the back of the shelf, to be brought out only for special occasions. But there is a final, wonderful irony – the kind of irony that mass-communication industries throw up from time to time. 'Reality' will live on and grow within a genre that was designed to be artificial – LIVE SPORT. This has evolved to be the only television genre which is real. The Beckham free kick against Greece, a moment of triumph or disaster, the most honestly real moment in this millennium, close up, heart-stopping. Like a medium-rare, juicy steak.

Essay Two

MONEY SHOT
Victoria Mapplebeck

> Now and then someone would accuse me of being evil – of letting people destroy themselves while I watched, just so I could film or tape record them. But I don't think about myself as evil – just realistic.
>
> Andy Warhol, quoted in Mike Wrenn,
> *Andy Warhol in His Own Words*, (Omnibus Press) 1991

Warhol wasn't evil. He was just fascinated by looking, and by people. Combine the two and you have his movies. Up in The Factory, he stood watching as his motley crew of stars bared their souls, his camera rolled as they had sex, fought and wept. Warhol was just as happy with the downtime: he also stood transfixed as he filmed his stars sleeping, eating or just sitting pretty. If he could have, he would have filmed them 24/7.

He would have loved Reality TV for its 'access all areas' approach to life. TV shows that don't stop, that enable you to get online and watch these new TV stars around the clock. Not only can you view them all hours, you can interact with them too. You can become a star of the show you consume. Truly 3-DTV. He would have been a big fan and no stranger to the controversy these shows invariably attract. Warhol was well used to the ubiquitous critical hype that comes when cameras go up close and personal. 'Weigh them, don't read them,' he said of his reviews. The hype was part of the event.

I have been there too. I wrote and directed *Smart Hearts*, one of Channel 4's first forays into Reality TV. The series received plenty of press, good and bad. *Smart Hearts* is a five-part documentary and online portrait of two friends of mine, Brendan Quick and Claire de Jong. It was TV's first documentary convergence series, featuring stories and characters that cross from TV to the net and back again. *Smart Hearts* combined my filming of the subjects with constant webcam access which streamed from the subjects' homes on to the *Smart Hearts* website. *Smart Hearts* was about life, lived, live for 18 months.

The series took as its starting point the roller-coaster of documentary access and consent. What happens when your private life goes public? This was Reality TV from the subject's point of view. As well as providing 3-D access, *Smart Hearts* explored the fall out. *Smart Hearts* takes its name from a Japanese Tamagotchi that bleeps when it finds your urban soul mate. The initial idea was to make a longitudinal series exploring a contemporary relationship. This was the late 1990s and everywhere you looked TV was obsessing about relationships. From *Trisha* to *Ally McBeal*, this perceived relationship meltdown was reduced to the adolescent vocabulary of *Bridget Jones*. All men feared commitment and all women were begging for it.

I wanted to explore with one couple, the complexities of changing attitudes to dating, marriage and having kids. Several relationship docusoaps had featured cartoon sad cases limping from one dating crisis to the next. I wanted to make the antidote. As well as filming over an 18-month period, I also wanted to use new technologies to consolidate this approach to increased access and intimacy. Researching online documentary for *Smart Hearts*, I'd spent a lot of time on webcam sites. Couple cam, family cam, dorm cam: the list goes on and on. In the *Independent*, David Aaronovitch said of the medium, 'Webcams ... allow the terminally bored to entertain the fatally bored' (9 August 2001).

True, the subjects can be boring. But the access is not. No matter how dull the subject, I could sit happily for hours watching real time families eating their cereal and arguing over the TV. These sites were all about the viewers' gaze. The focus was put back on looking; the relief of being able to watch rather than be told. No voice-over, no editing. And so I put the gaze of the webcams into the mix. The *Smart Hearts* subjects' homes would be live online for a year from the pilot's broadcast. Viewers could watch the emotional highs and lows of the subjects throughout production. They could interact with them to boot. Channel 4 liked it. Now we just had to find the subjects.

We put an advertisement in *Time Out*: 'Do you want to share with someone the roller coaster of your relationship, how about the entire nation?' To my amazement we had a good response. This was pre-*Big Brother* but post-*Jennicam*. The webcam sites seemed to have had a real influence on the access subjects were now prepared to provide. Many could deliver on the access but not the content. The people who responded to our advertisement led my producer Peter Day to conclude, 'the people who want to be on TV shouldn't be.'

I was forced to draw on my own life. I approached Brendan, an artist mate of mine, married to another artist Claire. I had a hunch they would be difficult, but good. My initial phone call reached Claire. Brendan was AWOL, having just left after their first and only session of marriage guidance counselling. Hearing they had split, I felt it was a case of back to the drawing board, but Brendan said he'd still be interested. Gradually they both came on board with varying degrees of enthusiasm. Filming a portrait of a broken marriage would have been a difficult and complex situation at the best of times. Add to that my constant filming of them and webcams streaming 24 hours a day, and this was a full on pride-swallowing siege for all concerned.

Brendan and Claire would not have agreed to filming if they hadn't been offered complete editorial control. To offer it is pretty much unheard of in documentary. Given the levels of access, I didn't think I had much choice. Nothing went in the series and the website that they hadn't already approved. This level of control was much like handing them a loaded gun, which they aimed at me on a regular basis.

Traditionally, documentary filmmakers have referred to the Stockholm Syndrome, in which the hostage falls for his/her kidnapper, to describe the apocryphal dependency subjects are supposed to have on their director. For me it was the reverse, I was their hostage for 18 months. Reality TV covers a multitude of sins. For me the definition is simple, it includes any documentary in which the format is clearly fore-grounded. Reality TV creates an obviously artificial environment, places the subjects in it, and records the results. Within the industry, the genre is also referred to as 'manipulated observational documentary'. Nothing new there – all documentary is manipulated. But Reality TV puts the artifice and agendas of traditional documentary on open display.

Smart Hearts was an authored, rather than a commercial approach to the genre. We had no phone votes, or prize money. However, webcams in the subjects' living room are a clearly artificial presence. So Reality TV it was. Reviewers of *Smart Hearts* loved it or loathed it. We were introduced by *Time Out* as, 'a radical collaborative piece of art' (30 August 2000). The *Guardian* previewed the series as, 'really hypnotic stuff' (30 August 2000), but we had plenty of the run for the hills variety of criticism: the *Daily Telegraph* hoped we would, 'help give Reality TV a bad name' (30 August 2000).

Reality TV raises the inevitable questions when cameras access the highs and lows of real lives. Is this reality or spectacle – surveillance or exhibitionism? Are these new subjects martyrs or stars?

REALITY OR SPECTACLE?

Who needs images of the world's otherness when we can watch these half persons enacting ordinary life?

> Salman Rushdie on British *Big Brother*,
> The *Guardian*, 9 June 2001

Documentary filmmakers have been endlessly preoccupied with a social and political panorama of the world. The world's 'otherness' that Salman Rushdie prioritizes over 'ordinary life'. Filmmakers have too often used the lens as a journalistic device rather than a cinematic one. Documentary had to be about fore-grounding issues over people, telling us rather than showing us. TV documentary often felt like an illustrated lecture. Once documentary focused almost exclusively on the problems in public institutions: in politics, in housing, in health care, in policing. Following the shift from public to private, epitomized by the talk shows, documentaries are now almost exclusively about personal rather than public crisis.

Documentary has always been about looking, but unlike any other lens-based media it has spent a great deal of energy disguising the fact. The online documentary gaze has changed all that. The constant close-ups of the webcam sites have put the emphasis fully back on spectacle. These sites emphasize rather than disavow the documentary gaze.

SURVEILLANCE OR EXHIBITIONISM?

Richard Brown, a radio reviewer of *Smart Hearts*, said of the access provided by the subjects, 'I braced myself for voyeuristic detail …

voyeuristic it wasn't: with voyeurism, you the viewer spy on the subject who is unaware of your presence ... The people we were watching wanted to be seen ... I didn't feel like a voyeur at all' ('The Message', BBC Radio 4, 8 August 2000).

'Voyeurism' constantly eludes a precise definition. It is used to cover a multitude of sins. Traditionally, voyeurism refers to the unacknowledged gaze, but the viewer's gaze in Reality TV is very much acknowledged. The subjects of Reality TV know they are being watched and they want to be. And yet, 'voyeuristic', is the endless battle cry of the Reality TV reviewer. It seems the consensual access subjects provide for Reality TV cameras has been mistakenly linked to the erosion of privacy in the non-consensual world of surveillance and electronic monitoring, as new digital technologies are providing a platform of wider and faster access to previously hidden areas of public life.

The once 'private' scandals of politicians, monarchs and celebrities are now played out like global soap operas. This kind of access is rarely consensual. Monica Lewinsky did not consent to the FBI accessing her private emails. Bill Clinton did not consent to the details of his sexual encounters being published online. American theorists Jeffrey Rosen and Clay Calvert have explored and criticized the increase in celebrity exposé, surveillance and electronic monitoring. Both are professors in law and examine the rise of electronic voyeurism, lamenting the erosion of privacy and the civil liberties of the subjects exposed.

In *Voyeur Nation: Media, privacy and peering in modern culture* (Westview Press, 2000), Clay Calvert is particularly critical of the rise of Reality TV, 'Discussion is replaced by watching. Indeed the flipside of the death of discourse is, I argue, the birth of voyeurism.' Many critics have worried about the 'death of discourse'. They lament the decline of the issue documentary. Documentary that could change the world. It is a TV hypochondria. The starting point for Reality TV is that the world has changed. Traditional documentary has on the whole failed to reflect these changes. The emphasis of Reality TV is unashamedly on the personal, on ethics rather than politics. This shift is seen by traditionalists as 'dumbing down', as exploitative, and as a corruption of the documentary tradition.

In all of this hand wringing, the critics miss the obvious point about new levels of access. This is not *The Truman Show*. These subjects haven't discovered the cameras, they have actively sought them out. The access these subjects have provided is consensual. They are aware of the cameras' gaze, the hum of the lighting rig. They meet that gaze, sometimes with a head butt.

MARTYRS OR STARS?

> Fucking mental and physical breakdown, all on TV ...
> Brendan Quick, Episode Two, *Smart Hearts*)

Smart Hearts was about looking and therefore about access. What made this series different from any other is that the usual levels of documentary access had been radically increased. The repercussions of this access were not disguised. The subjects denied access as much as they provided it. Brendan and his new girlfriend Lisa regularly went on webcam strike. This would invariably be just at the moment our commissioner was demonstrating the webcams to the head of Channel 4.

Instead of live and sensational access to a 3-D relationship lab, all they got on 'Brendan cam' was a shot of an Eastend corner shop. When Brendan got fed up, he'd hang the webcams out of his window. Fortunately, Claire loved the webcams and was on all day and night. She developed her own web audience and fan base. Viewers could watch her paint, cook, sleep and entertain. At one stage Leos Carax, director of the film *Pola X*, found her in cyberspace and got his casting director to track down her phone number.

But the critics worried. *Smart Hearts*, because of its increased access, was used by broadsheet TV critics as an example of the perceived ethical meltdown and moral decline of Channel 4. Yvonne Roberts' assumption in the *Independent*, that increased access automatically leads to increased exploitation, was fairly typical of the critical response to the series. 'Channel 4's new season includes *Smart Hearts*, "a multi media experiment to record the trials and tribulations of a modern marriage recorded over a twelve month period" ... Wow. An educational opportunity for us to learn from the mistakes of others or, emotional disembowelling, leaving (some) viewers queasy and the participants degraded?' (7 February 2000).

When I met Yvonne Roberts at a conference we were both speaking at, she admitted she hadn't seen *Smart Hearts*. This is a common feature of contemporary TV criticism. Critics regularly review the press release rather than the programme. Roberts, having not seen the series, was unaware that the project was collaborative, that the subjects had full editorial control and that they were keen to work on a second series. When Claire was asked by one of the audience in the chatrooms, 'How do you cope with your personal life being constantly on camera?', she responded, 'Frankly, I don't think its public enough.'

Although *Smart Hearts* was pitched as the antidote to the docu-soap, we were still stuck with its legacy. A decade of 'factual entertainment' had created a culture of viewers and critics who had grown used to a cast of happy losers prepared to let their lives descend into sitcom farce. Brendan and Claire didn't fit the bill. Brendan in particular paid the price.

The docusoap subjects were presented as mad, bad or sad. The online chat audiences tended to side with Claire as 'sad'; she was seen as the apocryphal abandoned wife. Brendan was just 'bad', as a hard drinking philanderer he was cast as the pantomime villain. Brendan complained, 'I'm horrified at being identified as the bloke who drinks in the mornings.' His girlfriend Lisa responded, 'That's your role in the movie ... the drunk from hell with no talent whatsoever, other than pulling pretty women' (Episode Five).

Even the broadsheet critics reviewed the subjects rather than the programmes. Polly Vernon in *The Guardian*, harked back to the perceived innocence of the docusoap A list. She said of *Smart Hearts*, 'The middle classes do not make good TV. As the title implies Brendan and his friends are becoming too smart about their programmes.' If being 'too smart' makes you a bad documentary subject, does being stupid make you a good one? Nostalgic for the comic and innocent pleasures of *Hotel* and *Airport*, Vernon continued, 'I like docusoaps. I don't think that says anything too awful about me – will the head chef at Burger King Stansted airport, cope with the disgruntled passengers from Malaga? Brilliant. It is a gentle form of voyeurism' (21 December 1999).

No, *Smart Hearts* is not a 'gentle form of voyeurism'. In terms of looking and access it was on the hardcore shelf – next to *Big Brother*.

BIG BROTHER: **MAN-MADE CRISIS**

The docusoap proved we love a loser. The *Big Brother* format merely turned the volume up on the documentary impulse to find us one. The crisis formula was man-made. Instead of waiting for the archetypal documentary scenes of exhibitionism, conflict, drama and tears, *Big Brother* openly engineered them. Endemol, the creators of *Big Brother*, began with a high-pressure environment of penal chic in which subjects were given few physical or psychological comforts. They've now turned the volume up.

Recently, the Dutch Endemol producers came up with *Big Brother: The Battle*, a reworking of the original *Big Brother* format. In terms of increasing the show's access there was nowhere to go. Instead the producers introduced more of the physical deprivations of the survival shows, such as *Castaway* and *Survivor*. The main *Big Brother* house has had an upgrade. The habitat sofas have been replaced with leather ones, house mates are treated to wide screen TVs and champagne on ice. But at the bottom of the garden sits the *Big Brother* shed. Here the housemates sleep on straw and live on baked beans.

Now the success or failure in the tasks can either upgrade you to the house or keep you and your team in the shed another three days. Imagine how this adds to the pressure. Lose a task and your team-mates will really hate you. The tears and fights must have doubled and for *Big Brother* this is the point. The battle format has proved so successful, a softcore version has been introduced into series three of British *Big Brother*. The series has become a 24/7 relationship laboratory. It explores contemporary ethics, the relationships between the individual and the group.

In Britain, these ethical dilemmas often centred not just on how the housemates related to each other, but also how they relate to authority, to Big Brother himself. One of the Australian *Big Brother* producers described the format as, 'a living soap in which the subjects write the script' (International Journal of Cultural Studies, Volume 4, Number 4, December 2001). This should give them more control. Conrad Green, the series producer of British *Big Brother*, feels the new formats of Reality TV have radically transformed the relationship between subject, producer and audience: 'I, as the producer, can intervene only a certain amount. The people in the house can determine their fate to a certain point, and the audience controls things but not completely ... At the core of it, there's a unique tension, a triangle of control' (*The Guardian*, 5 November 2001). And yet the British subjects, rather than exploiting their newfound power, on the whole ignored it. They were still pacified by the fall out of the docusoap and the British class system, both designed to keep subjects firmly in their place.

The finest moment of subject mutiny was when Nick Bateman broke the rules. Being the only public school boy among them, he was the obvious candidate. He had attempted to influence the housemates' nominations. Nick was exposed and punished. In the fantastically compelling eviction episode, the other housemates collectively brand him as a cheat and submit him to trial by TV. In Britain, Big Brother was Big Daddy. Meanwhile in international runs of *Big Brother* the housemates regularly gave Big Brother the runaround. In Denmark, all nine housemates mutinied. After having a party on the roof they decided they'd had enough and simply went home. *Big Brother* was forced to shut down for the day, the cameramen had nothing but the Habitat sofas to focus on. The producers had to track down the subjects and could persuade only three of them to return, on the condition that they could have weekly visits from their friends and family.

In South Africa when 'Bad Brad' tried to leave by the front door, it was locked so he began to unscrew the back gate. Big Brother tells him over the loud speaker this is unacceptable and he must return to the house. At this point the British subjects would have returned, pistol-whipped, back to sofas, providing the obligatory tear full close-up. Not Brad. He storms into the diary room and screams at Big Brother, 'I'm not your fucking hostage, your playmate, your puppet. Your rules, Big Brother, not mine. Open this fucking door or I'll knock it down.'

And back in Britain there's hell to pay because Nick has attempted a very poor bit of electioneering. 'You're so sick,' Darren says as he confronts Nick. 'Yes, you're so sick,' the rest of the housemates chorus. After what seems like hours of real time humiliation, he responds: 'It's a game show, it's a game! One has to do the best one can with it.' Nick retreats to the bedroom and breaks down. The cameras zoom in. This close-up of Nick Bateman in tears is now a TV icon. He was a broken man, emotionally undressed as he clung to his suitcase. To this day, I have not seen a documentary subject so exposed in such a sensational way. Watched first live on the web, in 24 hours it became the biggest web event the UK had ever seen.

The next day, the TV audience had also increased to seven million viewers. Just those extra few seconds of Nick unmasked was all it took. No voice-over, nothing to distract the viewer, you are looking at a man stripped aware to his lowest point, broken and unmasked and live to the nation. First that hit, then a few seconds on and you are beginning to think about the camera's gaze. This is a close-up that holds up a mirror to the audience. How does this make you feel? More silence. All there is to look at, is that face. For TV, this gaze is so long and still, it resonates. This is emotional pornography with an IOU. You the viewer are implicated. This is 3-D angst, not the soft focus crisis of the docusoap. No fake sympathy from a celebrity voice-over to get us off the hook.

I decided I wanted to meet Nick. He agreed to let me film him back up at the *Big Brother* house for a Film Four short I was making on his breakdown episode. I liked him. Not only did he seem extremely well versed in the victim voyeurism of popular documentary, he seemed uncritical and unfazed by it. When I asked him whether he felt degraded crying in front of seven million viewers, he responded cheerfully, 'The editors had to make the programme entertaining, and if someone's crying on national TV, what better soup to serve out to the public than someone at their weakest emotional point ... There's no point showing us all laughing ... They have to show friction, discord ... When people are very upset, that's when *Big Brother* is interesting, they strip people down to their bare necessities.'

Nick Bateman represents a new generation of viewers and potential subjects who understand the formulas and archetypes of Reality TV as much as the programme makers. Subjects almost seem willing to collude in the obligatory crisis moments and caricature. When Kathyrn Flett of the *Observer* watched his tears, there was more soul searching. 'Was this pain or pleasure? ... I watched the Friday night show with a *Big Brother* virgin. "This is horrible. Horrible. I hate this." But we remained glued, because there's no doubt the show brings out the car crash voyeur in us all' (20 August 2000). The obligatory car crash tag.

When Nick was still in the house, he attempted to get the sympathy vote from the housemates by telling them a fake sob story about his girlfriend having died in a car crash. Andrew Antony of the *Observer* said of the fiction, 'It was untrue, but his story brilliantly satirised the false sentiments of our confessional age, sentiments that have been painfully conspicuous among the rest of the cast' (13 August 2000). Reality TV is both informed by and influences the world outside its walls. *Big Brother* was built on the 'sentiments of a confessional age', the boom in first person media, epitomized by the talk shows.

This spectacle of crisis and confession has been around for decades. What may have been so transgressive about the close-up of Nick's tears, is that he is a bloke. The spectacle of pain and dysfunction has been traditionally a female affair. Whether it be talk shows, documentary, drama or news and current affairs, we are obsessed by the theatre of female pain. We haven't seen Prince Charles or Bill Clinton cry in public, but we have seen their wives and mistresses weep in glorious close-up. Diana wept for the BBC and Monica Lewinsky broke down for HBO. They cry, we love them. Gagged for two years, when Monica recently recounted her part in the Clinton scandal, she broke down several times. When she became so emotional she was unable to speak, a woman member of the televized audience shouted, 'We're on your side Monica.' The audience cheered in support. A guy later stood up and said to her, 'This is self serving and self supporting drivel, more about you and your pain and not about your own agency in making this happen.' The rest of the audience talked him back down. They'd paid good money to see her pain.

In America, where this confession fest began, female crisis and confession still receives pretty much collective sympathy. In Britain, however, the sympathy factor is outweighed by access guilt. We still want these money shots but in Britain they are mixed with contempt for those providing the access in the first place.

FAME SHAME

Publicity is like eating peanuts – once you start you can't stop.
Andy Warhol, quoted in Mike Wrenn,
Andy Warhol in His Own Words, 1991

Jeffrey Rosen, in *Unwanted Gaze: The Destruction of Privacy in America* (Random House, 2000), discusses American attitudes to milking your 15 minutes of fame. 'Being on TV is now seen as important as being a good citizen... Bill Clinton showed that in a culture of exposure, shamelessness is a self defence, no amount of bad behaviour is embarrassing as long as you appear on TV.' But this is Britain: on this side of the Atlantic your fame is also your shame.

The *Big Brother* micro stars were constantly on the receiving end of these double standards. Within weeks of the show finishing, the *Sun* demanded, 'Please leave our lives immediately. Your fifteen minutes of fame are up. You are not celebrities, you just happened to be part of a TV freak show which is now over. You are spoiling the memory of *Big Brother*. Go back to your jobs. We don't care about you anymore' (quoted in *The Guardian*, 7 July 2001). British celebrities must provide access while simultaneously appearing to deny it. If they fail to play the martyr, they will pay the price. It is simply not British to exploit your fame. It exists to exploit you. The roles cannot be reversed.

This point was particularly evident when the doors closed behind Vanessa Feltz and Anthea Turner on *Celebrity Big Brother*. Within what seemed like minutes, it was tears before bedtime. Clearly the producers were rubbing their hands in glee. *Big Brother* had got its money shot without the usual foreplay. This really was fast-track breakdown. The tears seemed such a formulaic *Big Brother* moment, you couldn't help but wonder whether this was an elaborate mock documentary parody. Vanessa got no sympathy but plenty of column inches. The *Sun* reckoned she was as, 'mad as a hatter' (25 March 2001). And the *Daily Mail*, 'a squawking, pouting deflated balloon of a B grade celebrity' (25 March 2001). Barbara Ellen in the *Observer* concluded that, 'The theatrical blabbing of Feltz and Turner gave rise to the feeling that this was not so much Reality TV, as much as it was Priory TV' (18 March 2001). If Vanessa had wept outside a courtroom, or outside her therapist's, she would have been fine, but in the *Big Brother* house the access you provide is seen as so self-serving and shameful that even tears won't get you off the hook. Reality TV, confession culture and tabloid hype are on a constant loop. A cyclical exchange, one feeds into another and back again.

In January 2001, Alan and Judith Kilshaw found themselves at the centre of an adoption scandal which ran like a global soap opera. I spent the next six months filming them for a documentary for Channel 4. I was attracted to their story. It was clear that the tabloid narratives and hype of Reality TV had now infiltrated news and current affairs. Now, news figures are judged as if there is an audience phone vote. As Tim Allen said in the *Observer*, 'The grand tabloid narratives, like the Kilshaws or Monica Lewinsky... require us to condemn as well as to sympathise, and like all stories, they need a beginning, a middle and an end... Clearly real and complex lives are shrunk to fit' (27 January 2002).

The press dubbed the Kilshaws the worst parents in Britain. The *Sun* claimed, 'Judith wasn't fit to tend a house plant' (January 2001) and Tony Blair described their actions as 'deplorable'. The Kilshaws were falsely accused of adopting a baby over the internet. In fact, they had gained information about overseas adoption on the internet. The story was so hyped by the red tops you would have thought the Kilshaws had gone online, put in their credit card details and received a baby back by Fedex. Tony Blair, ever playing to the tabloid gallery, said defiantly in Parliament, 'This deplorable internet baby trade must be stopped' (January 2001).

There is no internet baby trade. The only crime Judith Kilshaw committed was being working class and loud. The Kilshaws had a much easier ride on *Oprah*. In America the Kilshaws were the victims. The villain of the piece was a corrupt system of private adoption which needed regulating. In Britain, the more the Kilshaws attempted to set the records straight, the worse it got. Judith was constantly hassled for interviews by the media who then attacked her for giving them.

We are now encouraged to look at news stories for their soap opera potential. We judge the subjects of these stories in terms of their likeability. If this had been fast-track celebrity *Big Brother*, the Kilshaws would have been out on the bridge of shame on day one. As Jeffrey Rosen concludes of the pitfalls of 'shrink to fit' celebrity gossip, 'As intimate information about our lives is increasingly recorded, archived and made hard to delete, there is a growing danger that a part of our identity will be confused with the whole of our identity... We confuse information with knowledge' (*Unwanted Gaze*, 2000).

Meet the Kilshaws received good viewing figures even though, ironically, it was up against the last episode of *Survivor*. My aim was to provide a portrait of the Kilshaws as an antidote to increasing tabloid caricature. It worked. No longer 'the wicked witch of the web', the reviewers turned. *The Times* described Judith as, 'a fabulous character' (26 July 2001) and the *Mail* as, 'a born performer with star quality ... larger than life with a mad maniacal courage' (1 August, 2001). It takes a 'mad maniacal courage' to deal with the fall out of 3-D access to your personal life.

CONCLUSION

There has been a great deal of speculation that, post 11 September 2001, the machiavellian formats of contemporary media will lose favour. Nice will become the new nasty. This isn't the answer either. There are only so many repeats of *Little House on the Prairie* and *Friends* the viewing public can take. Grief, conflict and crisis are a part of our identity and our experience. These emotions are the stuff of melodrama. Melodrama can be good or bad. It ranges from the worst of daytime soaps to the best of Douglas Sirk. What is new is that the conflict and crisis of melodrama are being increasingly sought by documentary, news and Reality TV cameras.

The key point is how these emotional climaxes are represented. The point of *Smart Hearts* was to look and to ask how we look. To challenge why when documentary goes up close and personal, it has always been about the backward glance rather than the full-on gaze. Predictably, most critics were shocked by the level of access in *Smart Hearts*. Reviews would acknowledge the compulsiveness of this intimacy but invariably attach a prefix of guilt. 'Compulsively compelling', one critic said, 'morbidly fascinating' said another. 'Car crash TV' came up in several reviews. I always felt it was over the top, such an obvious example of journalese.

In Reality TV, viewers are not peering at death and mayhem: they are merely watching how people behave behind closed doors. In porn, the money shot marks the end of a scene, the punch line. Warhol caught these emotional climaxes, but they weren't his money shots. In Warhol films, emotional highs and lows were merely part of the bigger portrait. The best of innovative documentary includes these moments of melodrama as the starting point, not the punch line. The increased access and spectacle of Reality TV has bought documentary into the twenty-first century. Subjects and viewers are now part of the equation. It has woken them up.

I'll leave the final comment on the pitfalls and potential of Reality TV to Brendan. In one of the *Smart Hearts* live chats, Brendan was asked if he would like to become a docusoap micro celebrity, like the women from *Cruise*. He replied, 'I know who I am, I don't need to join a fucking celebrity morgue.' He signed out of the chat room with, 'Don't let this programme degenerate into who you like ... Let the excesses of documentary, the dramatic moments of editing, let that tell you what TV is, because I can't' (*Smart Hearts* website: www.the-loop.com/smarthearts).

Essay Three

IT'S NOT NEW AND IT'S NOT CLEVER
Christopher Dunkley

Most of the claims made for 'Reality TV' are either highly questionable or demonstrably false. Take, for a start, the assertion, made repeatedly by many of those responsible for the best known examples, that this is something quite new to television. Among the most heavily hyped series to be shown in the UK was *Castaway 2000*, the BBC series in which 35 volunteers were to be left – supposedly – to fend for themselves for 12 months like the Swiss Family Robinson, on the remote Scottish island of Taransay in the Outer Hebrides. Cameras would show their efforts to survive and what sort of social structures developed, whether the castaways promptly re-invented democracy and the parish council, or descended into vicious hostilities, like the children in *Lord Of The Flies*. It would, we were told, be 'a unique social experiment'.

However, viewers with good memories may have wondered just how unique it was, given that 22 years earlier John Percival had produced a BBC series called *Living In The Past* in which a group of volunteers undertook to live as iron age settlers for 12 months, with cameras watching their efforts to survive and create their own pecking order. It seems that Percival got the idea from an even earlier programme in which cameras had observed a group left to their own devices in the middle of Exmoor, where they had to survive on available resources. And that was preceded in the 1950s, when television was in its infancy, by an experiment undertaken by the BBC for a history series in which cameras recorded the activities of a group of volunteers who had been left to survive on a remote island. Where? Off the coast of Scotland, it seems.

In the spring of 2001, just over a year after *Castaway 2000*, the BBC came up with another brilliant 'new' Reality TV idea: they would advertise for volunteers to live as iron age settlers, their efforts to survive and form their own social structures being recorded by television cameras for a series to be called *Surviving The Iron Age*. As with *Castaway 2000*, which had quickly collapsed into farce as grumpy volunteers scuttled back to the comfort of hotels and supermarkets on the mainland, complaining that Taransay's heating and lavatories were not up to scratch, this hoary old 'new' idea rapidly turned into a fiasco as today's softies proved hopelessly incapable of fulfilling the most basic tasks. Attempting to cook chicken stew they poisoned themselves, and when they tried to wipe their bottoms with the leaves growing closest to their earth closet, they discovered too late that the plants were stinging nettles.

It might be argued that these are exactly the sorts of result that a good Reality series ought to throw up, showing that in the twenty-first century we lack the most fundamental skills of our ancestors. But a more compelling argument is that slick and cynical journalism was merely exploiting ignorance for the sake of entertainment. It is entirely predictable that people who have neither been raised in primitive conditions like real iron age folk, nor taught necessary survival skills by the programme makers, will come to grief the moment they are thrown into iron age conditions. What *Surviving The Iron Age* illustrated most vividly was that Reality TV has more to do with entertainment, humiliation, and the scramble for ratings than with serious journalism or any genuine search for social insights.

◆ ● ●
● ●
● ● ◆ **VAGUELY FAMILIAR?**

Castaway 2000 began in the spring of 2000 but it was not the first in this recent era to feature survival in challenging circumstances. In the autumn of 1999, Channel 4 had shown *The 1900 House* and had been surprised and pleased at the success of what they had assumed might be a series of rather specialized interest. In the event, a remarkably large audience by Channel 4's standards kept coming back to watch the efforts of the 'real' and 'ordinary' Bowler family to survive in a Victorian terraced house under Victorian conditions: cooking on a coal-fired range, reading by candlelight and washing their hair in home made shampoo. The popularity of the series gave rise to an entire sub-genre of Reality TV with Channel 4 subsequently applying the same formula to a family living in World War Two conditions, complete with rationing and 'Utility' goods, and then, in 2002, the BBC sending volunteers to live in trenches modelled precisely on those of World War One.

The claim that we are witnessing something entirely new to television proves hardly any more accurate when you look at another group of 'reality' programmes which developed in parallel to the survival-in-difficult-circumstances strand. The intention of *Popstars*, launched by ITV in January 2001, was '… to develop and launch a hit all-UK pop band from scratch'. Doesn't that also sound vaguely familiar? It should to anyone old enough to remember *The Monkees*. Television developed and launched that group from scratch as a hit pop band in 1966, the difference being that, because it was done by NBC in the United States, the members of the group were, largely, American, though David Jones was an English jockey. The Monkees also differed from ITV's 2001 group (which ended up being called Hear'Say) in that none of them had learned to sing or play an instrument, a fact which may sound crucial, but in the event proved, interestingly, to be of no significance whatsoever.

There was one other important difference. Whereas the American series *began* with the group coming to the screen fully formed after 400 hopefuls had been auditioned and whittled down to the final four away from the cameras, 35 years later in Britain the audition process itself was the main selling point of the series which *ended* with the formation of the group. *Popstars* proved immensely popular, giving ITV some of its biggest ratings of the season, and providing the main reason for including this type of programme under the 'reality' banner. The wannabes were 'real' in the special sense of the word as used by television: they came overwhelmingly from what used to be called the lower-middle and working classes (or, to those in advertising, socio-economic categories C2, D and E). And what you saw was 'real' in the sense that hopelessly bad performers were told to their faces just how dreadful they were by the panel of judges in front of an audience of millions. It was, of course, the judges who acquired celebrity status during the run of the series, though, as the organizers had planned, Hear'Say did indeed have a No 1 hit shortly after being declared the winners, by which time they were well on the way to becoming minor celebs.

It may be objected that this difference between *The Monkees* and *Popstars* – the formation of the group marking the beginning of the former series but the end of the latter – negates the assertion that there is nothing very new about this branch of so-called Reality TV. However, it was not merely in the creation of a pop group by television that ITV was relying on a well-tried formula. In using the auditioning process as its chief element, *Popstars* was following in an even more firmly established tradition: the talent contest. From *Opportunity Knocks* in the 1950s to *Stars In Their Eyes* today, there has scarcely been a time when British television has been without a talent show. Among the most famous was ITV's *New Faces* which ran on and off from 1973 to 1988, becoming notorious for the way in which unsuccessful contestants were told, in front of millions, just how dreadful they were. What the brutally frank record producer and *New Faces* judge Mickie Most had been to the 1970s, the brutally frank pop producer and *Popstars* judge Nigel Lythgoe was to 2001: loved and loathed as the most outspoken member of the panel.

A third group of Reality TV programmes comprised sophisticated modern versions of what Boy Scouts call wide games: individuals or teams rushing around the landscape, against the clock, attempting to accomplish detailed tasks laid down by the organizers. Pretty clearly, the origins lay in activities such as treasure hunts and hare-and-hounds contests. A typical example, *The Mole*, was launched by Channel 5 in the same week in January 2001 that ITV started *Popstars*. The idea was that ten people, selected from the thousands who answered newspaper advertisements, went off together to some unidentified foreign island to undertake challenges, both mental and physical, the accomplishment of which would put tens of thousands of pounds into a kitty. Each week one contestant was dropped and the last to survive took all the cash. To add to the difficulties, the contestants were told that one of them was a 'mole' inserted by the producers to sabotage the efforts of the others, though they didn't know who – hence the title.

So how new is that idea? Leaving aside series such as *Jailbreak* and *Fort Boyard*, both based upon the notion of teams facing challenges and both screened by Channel 5 not long before *The Mole*, you can trace the antecedents back through team contest programmes such as *The Crystal Maze* (studio-based but similar in atmosphere and approach to *The Mole*) via *Passport*, in which players flew to mystery locations to compete in challenges, mental and physical, to the 1980s' series *Interceptor* in which one contestant had the task of trying to sabotage the others. Above all you would look back to *Treasure Hunt*, the 'helicopter orientated adventure game' shown throughout most of the 1980s in which Kenneth Kendall stayed in the studio with members of the public to give instructions by radio to Anneka Rice who hared all over the landscape in speedboats, Landrovers, and helicopters, using cryptic, and sometimes not so cryptic, clues to track down the treasure. In *The Mole* they used mobile phones instead of radios, but otherwise the formula was remarkably similar: speedboats. Landrovers, helicopters, not so cryptic clues, the works.

Still, even if survival programmes, talent contests and treasure hunts were old hat, surely in creating the most notorious Reality TV series of all, *Big Brother*, the producers could say that – like Edison who gained fame as the inventor of the light bulb and gramophone even though his were refinements rather than first examples – this was different enough from any predecessors to be claimed as something really new? To be honest, no they could not. The idea of *Big Brother* was that ten young people would live together for nine weeks in a house where two dozen cameras and even more microphones would record everything they did. There would be one room with an unmanned camera where they could get away from one another and complain or confess to 'Big Brother', the anonymous producer, but otherwise they could be observed all over the house, even in the shower room and lavatory.

As with virtually all Britain's reality programmes, this formula had already been tried in other countries and proved successful. *Popstars* was an Australian format which also achieved big ratings in New Zealand before the British version was made; *The Mole* had been a success in several countries before the rights were bought for British production; and *Big Brother* had been a huge triumph in Holland, Germany, Spain and the US before a deal was done for a British version. However, it is not just on those grounds that the British *Big Brother* loses its claim to novelty. Seven years earlier in the autumn of 1993 the BBC decided it was time to build on the work done by Paul Watson in his fly-on-the-wall series *The Family*, which had closely observed the home life of the Wilkins family of Reading in 1974, and his much more recent *Sylvania Waters*, which paid similar up-yer-nostrils attention to Noelene Baker and her brood in the suburbs of Sydney.

Moving on from those celebrated series, the BBC set out to document every detail of the lives of six Manchester students, rigging up a house for them to share with umpteen cameras and microphones, and providing a room with an unmanned camera where they could get away from one another and confess or complain about their lives to the producers. True, the BBC did not whittle down the number of young people in the house by getting viewers to vote them out, but numbers fell anyway as the students discovered the horrors of living perpetually in the public eye. At that the BBC promptly organized a telephone poll to decide which of a number of wannabes should go *into* the house as replacements. In other words, this series, which they called *The Living Soap*, featured practically every important element of *Big Brother*.

IT'S A KNOCKOUT

It could be said, however, that the few factors in *Big Brother* which had not been pioneered by *The Living Soap* were the ones that mattered most: a big cash prize for the winner and regular humiliation as the other contestants were eliminated. As it happened, the BBC's earlier series, though not intended as a contest, did eventually evince some of the spirit of a competition when some students were seen to crumple under the strain while others survived, though that was never presented as being a very important ingredient. However, if anything sets apart Reality TV from previous television series, which were otherwise very similar, it is the significance of the part played by humiliation. Thus, the second false claim is that Reality TV is a serious form which emerged from documentary, history and travel series, the most important constituent being social insights. Far from being part of any serious factual programming tradition, as broadcasters like to pretend, these series are much more similar to and closely connected with game shows and, in particular, *It's A Knockout*, a BBC series which ran between 1966 and 1982 and was itself a descendent of the 1950s contest *Top Town*.

Generally speaking, the people who make game shows choose the contestants, invent the rules, dream up the silly tasks which have to be performed, award the points, decide on the winners, and dish out the prizes. It is a process tailored to the needs and wants of programme makers which could hardly be more different from a traditional observational documentary. It is not difficult to perceive a direct line of descent from the long-winded and long running *It's A Knockout* to series such as *Castaway 2000*, *The Mole* and even *Big Brother*. Documentary programme makers may stay with their subject for days, weeks, months, and even years (think of Adrian Cowell in the South American rainforest making *Decade Of Destruction*) but if they have integrity they go to great lengths to avoid the effects of the Heisenberg Uncertainty Principle – well, the popular version, anyway, which states that the act of observation distorts that which is being observed. One of the main concerns of proper documentary makers is to ensure that their own involvement has as little effect as possible on what they film, the intention being to show reality uncontaminated by television.

The makers of Reality TV on the other hand openly intervene from start to finish, fixing everything to suit their own ends. As with game shows they begin by auditioning far more people than will eventually be used, in order to be sure that they get the right kind of participants: entertaining types, good sports, show offs, and of course a sprinkling of the eccentric and bolshie to add spice. In *Popstars* this selection process, as we have seen, provided the main body of the series, but *Castaway 2000* also exploited the selection process to provide its first few programmes. We watched them split up scores of hopefuls into teams to put them through their paces, finding out who could co-operate, who would lead and who would follow, whether they were too squeamish to wring the neck of a live chicken, who had the best sense of humour, and so on.

Had the same sort of care not been taken in setting up a series such as *Survivor*, in which two teams were taken to a tropical island to play wide games and, supposedly, live off their wits, then instead of being merely a comparative failure, with ITV reduced to halving the number of programmes and moving most of the series out of peak time, it could have been a total disaster. As it was, *Survivor* was subjected to a good deal of ridicule thanks to its pretentiousness. The makers drafted in a former journalist to call the contestants to tribal gatherings and intone all sorts of new age psychobabble about fire symbolizing their lives on the island and so on, before getting them to vote in coconut shells on who should be next for the heave-ho. The competitive tasks they were given tended toward the spiteful: eating huge live white maggots; seeing who could stand for longest on the end of a log fixed upright in the lagoon without getting stiff or collapsing from boredom (hours and hours, about 18, I seem to remember), the kind of humiliating and ludicrous activities which made nonsense of any claims to serious social intentions. In ratings terms, the series was saved solely by the casting which did at least ensure that there was jealousy, sexual competition – no, no, nothing explicit, heaven forbid, this was British television don't forget – and plenty of rows, the very stuff that keeps soap operas perpetually at the top of the ratings.

So, if there is nothing very new about the structure of Reality TV programmes (interactivity? – it is scarcely a revolutionary change to vote to throw Nasty Nick out of the *Big Brother* house by using the buttons on your channel changer rather than the buttons on your phone) and if these series are obviously part of the entertainment sector of the industry rather than contributors in any significant way to television journalism, is there really nothing noteworthy about them at all? Have they acquired a peculiarly high publicity profile not because of any genuine originality or true value but because they provided a flood of the sort of material which happens to suit the red top newspapers down to the ground? There could be some truth in that.

The symbiotic relationship which sprang up between the red tops and some of these series was extraordinarily powerful. Day after day, piffling instances of flirtation, hostility or jealousy in the programmes were seized upon by the papers and blown up into front-page sagas. In particular, the smallest hint of any sexual relationship on screen could lead to entire pages of 'investigation' in the papers (complete with sexy pictures) of a sort which the programmes themselves could not or would not envisage. Thus, a virtuous circle was created in which the programmes provided subject matter for the tabloids, the follow-ups by the tabloids provided massive publicity for the programmes, and each medium ended up providing huge quantities of priceless promotion for the other.

DEBATING MATTERS

◆ ● ●
● ● **CONCLUSION – HUMILIATION TV:**
● ● ◆ **THE WORST IS STILL TO COME**

Yet there is one noteworthy innovation in Reality TV, and it is this business of being deliberately nasty and holding up members of the public to ridicule. Reality TV is not alone here: quiz shows such as *The Weakest Link* and unsuccessful copycat attempts including one on Channel 5 presented by the American Jerry Springer, *Greed*, and another from the BBC presented by Robert Kilroy-Silk, *Shafted*, have all set out to use scorn and contempt for the participants as selling points. But it is the reality shows that have gone to most trouble to work mockery and humiliation of the contestants into the very structure of their programmes. Yes, most involve some sort of competition so that there is inevitably a winner but, throughout most of the run of these series, they are far more preoccupied with losers.

That much-hyped interactivity on *Big Brother* consisted of viewers calling in to vote for the next contestant to suffer the ignominy of being chucked out of the house, once the occupants themselves had voted of course. So viewers were guaranteed the sight of one victim every week, first shown up as being the least popular among fellow competitors, then among the public. Nor was that the end. After emerging from the house, they had to go into another television studio to be interrogated on their failure. When the producers followed up their bog standard *Big Brother* with a celebrity version, it became clear that this sort of victimization can have a pretty disturbing effect upon people such as Vanessa Feltz and Anthea Turner, both C-list celeb television presenters, who went to pieces on screen at the mere prospect of being voted out. Perhaps they felt they had more to lose than the members of the public who had appeared in the original series – but whatever the reason they certainly reacted far more embarrassingly to rejection than those 'ordinary' contestants.

You could hardly mistake the intentions of the programme makers in choosing the tasks to be imposed on the competitors in *Survivor*, which put me in mind of a rather horrible game we used to play after dinner parties in the 1960s: how much cash would you demand to have certain parts of you surgically removed – one ear lobe, a little finger, and so on. In the case of *Survivor* the question was how much humiliation the participants would tolerate in order to continue with the chance of winning tens of thousands of pounds. Stand on a pillar all night surrounded by water? Okay. Bite the heads off big fat wriggling maggots? Well, all right ... The most vivid examples cropped up in *Popstars* and *Pop Idol* where some of the judges seemed to take a positive pleasure in disparaging the more pathetic wannabes. 'That used to be one of my favourite songs; not any more,' Simon Cowell told one competitor. To another he said, 'Did you have singing lessons? You should sue.'

We shall be told that all this is just a sign of the times, an inevitable part of a cynical age in which all types of personal belief – religious, political, social – have been swept away in a tidal wave of recent history that destroyed the last pathetic remnants of idealistic political societies and left us with nothing but the dog-eat-dog habits of the so-called free market. It is an interestingly facile explanation for the popularization of a type of television which has all the attractions of bear-baiting, the stocks and public hanging. And, judging from the way that previous sea changes in television have proceeded, anyone who thinks we have now seen the worst aspects of Reality TV – which might more accurately be called humiliation TV – almost certainly has another think coming.

Essay Four

FROM DIRECT CINEMA TO CAR-WRECK VIDEO: REALITY TV AND THE CRISIS OF CONTENT

Graham Barnfield

Reality TV is now a mainstay of the television schedules. As one commentator suggested, 'Such is the proliferation of the genre, it now appears impossible to indulge in a threesome, involve yourself in holiday promiscuity in Faliriki or have a pub fight these days without engaging with the star of a reality television show' (Jim White, 'Summer lovin', *G2*, 14 January 2002). Combining huge publicity with high ratings, reality shows have prompted a furious critical debate whilst becoming a cash cow for broadcasters and producers.

Current responses to Reality TV gel around several familiar themes. On the one hand, the genre is seen as part of 'dumbing down', offering a mixture of banality and emotional pornography. On the other hand, defenders of the genre point to its popular and democratic character, giving those on the margins unprecedented access to the airwaves. It appears that responses to such programmes are filtered through the outlooks and prejudices of a range of commentators. These divergent views are further complicated by the application of various technologies, from the webcam to CCTV. Technically, the reality genre can seem simultaneously open and intrusive because of the gadgetry permitting its creation (although usually someone has to agree to the installation of said kit in the first place). This heady mixture of taste, technology and diminished privacy can make for a confusing controversy.

Many complainants act as if they are dealing with an entirely new phenomenon. In Britain, the statistical gulf between votes cast for *Big Brother* and electoral turnout is taken to signal the triumph of Reality TV (not to mention the demise of politics). The recent telecommunications spending spree of *Pop Idol* viewers has tended to confirm these impressions. Each new ratings-buster is closely scrutinized by programme makers and searched for key features to incorporate into future productions. When UK broadcasters pondered the ratings triumphs of *Big Brother* over *Survivor* and their US counterparts did the reverse, it reflected an underlying preoccupation with potential audience figures. The networks' uncertainty reflects concerns about how best to deploy the new formats. Likewise, dazzled by such programmes' popularity, critics often treat the Reality TV boom as entirely novel. This ignores the continuities with earlier forms of non-fiction broadcasting.

TABLOID TV

Over a decade ago, the forerunners of 'tabloid television' were attracting some hostility in the United States. Opponents of network deregulation under the Reagan administration noted a definite link between the increasing incursion of market forces into an already highly commercial system and the declining quality and quantity of non-fiction in the schedules. Douglas Kellner outlined this process:

Whereas each network broadcast around 20 documentaries a year during the 1960s, by 1985 all three networks together were broadcasting a mere 14 hours worth. Instead, news magazines such as ABC's '20/20' and CBS' 'West 57th Street' appeared, along with 'reality programming' (sensationalistic tabloid journalism of the sort found in the New York *Daily News* or *Post*), including Geraldo Rivera's 'exposés' of satanism and live drug busts. In this way, political journalism turned towards a tabloid style of journalism and away from analysis and criticism.

'Television, the Crisis of Democracy and the Persian Gulf War', M. Raboy and B. Dagenais (eds), *Media, Crisis and Democracy: Mass Communication and the Disruption of the Social Order*, Sage, 1992.

It is striking that Kellner needed to use examples to explain to his readers what a reality show was. Today no such illustration would be necessary. It is also notable that his critique is directed primarily at a mixture of Republican policy makers and lobbyists, whose decisions allow in the trash. It is taken as read that tabloid journalism has no place alongside serious documentary; pointing out its increasing share of scheduling is an indictment of the state of the networks. To early 1990s' media malcontents, such trends were merely the backdrop to biased and uncritical coverage of events like the Gulf War; the 'reality programming' or 'tabloid television' needed no further comment since it was self-evidently substandard.

Nowadays the quotation marks are off. Use the labels and people will know instantly what is meant. This loose usage leaves the present essay faced with a terminological problem: over the last decade such a wide range of productions have been categorized as 'Reality TV' that one wonders if the term is too general to be helpful. The 'reality' label is applied to a wide range of television, from the shrieking, tearful guests on *Jerry Springer* to the grainy camcorder footage of *When Good Pets Turn Bad*. Indeed, 'reality' can span the divide between the long-term investigative findings of an undercover reporter and cut-price accident video anthologies (taking in *Pop Idol* along the way). In short, the phrase has become shorthand for distinguishing such material both from the current affairs and (openly) fictional output of various broadcasters. Treating it as a genre in its own right is confusing, but this is not to say 'Reality TV' doesn't exist.

Let's work with the assumption that there is a distinction between fiction and non-fiction productions. Granted, mentioning this difference fuels the reader's suspicions that 'reality' shows somehow overlap with and bleed into those other scheduling staples (not least when the near-ubiquitous handheld camera makes many dramas and sitcoms look like documentaries). The scope for an individual to ham it up for the cameras makes us approach each new show with some suspicion, and rightly so. Simultaneously, it grounds viewers in the cod universalism of asking 'what would I do in this situation?' Little wonder Germaine Greer tells us that 'Reality television is not the end of civilisation as we know it; it is civilisation as we know it' (cited in the *Observer*, 3 February 2002). She has a point, although more by accident than design.

Greer is replying to the commentators whose hostility suggests there is something substantial at stake here. When, outside of university media studies departments, did entertainment programming excite such strong views? To those who welcome such an apparently broad range of subject matter, ordinary folk on screen – *People Like Us*, as it were – are displacing the privileged exhibitionists, politicians and actors who would otherwise hog the wavelengths. Yet to the sceptics, Reality TV is as constructed, rehearsed and polished as any other form of mass entertainment, catering for voyeurs along the way. Both camps note the sacrifice of the old public service ethos, welcoming or condemning it, depending on a pre-established viewpoint. Yet as the controversy thunders on, a key point is missed: by confining the debate to one of broadcasting issues, few consider whether 'reality' itself has changed. Evidence of such a shift can be found in the way that altered public/audience values – towards privacy, modesty and self-respect, among other things – have created openings for reality television.

CHANGES IN THE REAL WORLD

Reality shows thrive at a time when all perspectives are seen as equally valid. Their admirers celebrate this, by pointing to the success of gays, lesbians and 'ordinary folk' like *Big Brother*'s Helen and Craig, as an indicator of more open-minded social attitudes. Can this easy-going relativism be linked to the demise of the public service ethos in television? Certainly reality shows have prospered whilst a consensus about what constitutes 'the public' has been in decline. Realistically there can be no return to the clarity of BBC pioneer Sir John Reith knowing what's good for us. Yet a significant theme amid the paternalism of old was one of self-improvement: in theory at least, the BBC once promised to take viewers outside the realm of their immediate experience. Nowadays such sentiments seem confined to the promotional blurbs for the BBC4 digital channel. Admittedly, no one wants the return of broadcasts prefaced with instructions on correct posture and room ventilation, which belong to an era of ventriloquists on the wireless and the Mercury Theatre's Martian invasion. Yet watching a slightly more exhibitionist version of yourself say that their 'biggest ever challenge' in life was getting on with their *Big Brother* housemates for a fortnight seems introspective, to say the least. Once the prospect of genuine self-improvement is cast out, all one is left with is entertainment, no matter how much of a celebration of ethnic diversity this entails.

Some seek to explain the shift to *Big* Brother as a metaphor for society in technical terms. In the digital and multi-channel environment of multi-set households, how can patterns of preferred viewing be established? The strategy of 'narrowcasting', of aiming to capture, say, the teenage audience whilst quietly giving up on the national one, has been widely accepted outside of peaktime schedules. Yet simultaneously the broadcasters search for elusive 'water cooler moments', when the previous night's TV becomes today's topic of workplace smalltalk. From temporal fetish to holy grail: this shift of focus reveals a hankering after some sort of common public experience.

Refracted through the bubbles of the water cooler, the viewers (or at least the ratings-collating BARB households) are now setting the agenda. Collectively, broadcasters pine for common experiences, but this represents a striking abdication of the authority once embodied in a figure like Reith. Whatever its faults, the public service model tried to base its output on what it intuited to be the common interests of a majority of listeners and viewers. The contemporary equivalent – pursuit of water cooler moments – entails aiming no higher than the perceived predilections of the viewing public. Moreover, as the latest antics from *Temptation Island* crawl into our TV sets, the channel chiefs have an alibi that rebounds upon the viewers: 'We're just giving them want they want.' If that includes *Pop Idol*, so be it. Such themes can shape the schedules thanks to a promiscuous relativism at the heart of contemporary society. Despite honourable exceptions to the broad outline offered below, it is apparent that any consensus as to the purpose of factual programming has broken down. This is reflected in the very organization of many shows or series: somewhat schematically, they shift from the top-down 1970s pedagogy of *The World at War*, via 1980s talking heads and oral history, to the present day where nothing historic ever happens to Reality TV participants (space does not permit an exploration of the continuing fascination with the Nazis on some channels: just how many of *Hitler's Henchmen* were there?). Even the shows which attempt to allow their participants to relive history – *Iron Age Family*, *The Trench* and *1900 House* – reveal that petty disputes flare up in these contrived circumstances (like at home) and that domestic chores and personal consumption were even more disheartening back then than they are now. Profound stuff. No doubt readers can object here by listing the excellent documentaries gracing our screens most weeks, many of which have coincided with the reality explosion. Yet these exceptions prove the rule, because we are already discussing documentary and entertainment in the same breath. Current intellectual trends make it both necessary and unpopular to uphold a distinction that was once seen as self-evident.

The idea of objective truth has been systematically undermined, with grave consequences for documentary. Such sentiments are expressed most sharply in academia, such as Bill Nichols's argument that the 'notion of any privileged access to a reality that exists "out there," beyond us, is an ideological effect. The sooner we realize all this, the better' (*Representing Reality: Issues and Concepts in Documentary*, Indiana University Press, 1991). Academics often amplify the slightest trace of audience scepticism. Acceptance of the concept of objective reality declines, undercutting part of documentary's reason for existence. In such circumstances, other forms of programme-making can exercise a more authoritative claim to represent some form of reality. Linked to the belief that the author is dead, the viewer or 'reader' of the televisual 'text' is free to construct his or her own reality from whatever materials are offered them. As I argue below, the discerning viewer is crucial, but this does not mean all forms of 'factual television' can be used to approximate and appropriate the world around us.

Docusoap narratives seem manufactured because they often are, yet every suspicion that they are all pre-planned pretence should be tempered by the sheer incoherence on show. In contrast to non-fiction programming with a purpose, a fragmented picture emerges from simple observations of everyday life. Life is like that, one may argue, but dealing exclusively in surface forms obstructs the emergence of detailed analysis. Bracketing reality programming with other factual output means that the question 'why' is posed – in television journalism style – with little hope of an answer. This is not a problem if the main objective is to entertain or look anarchic, but it militates against shedding new light on the topic at hand.

Now praised as a postmodern virtue, the fragmentary narrative was once seen as television journalism's main failing. As early as 1975, future BBC Chairman Marmaduke Hussey and co-author Peter Jay criticized the 'bias against understanding' arising from most TV journalism. Hussey's career was unharmed by his suggestion that broadcast news and current affairs were too often concerned with mere details at the expense of context, but such claims did little to rectify the situation (see Brian McNair, *News & Journalism in the UK*, Routledge, 1999). As the century drew to a close, 'other news' – the non-economic, non-political, non-sporting bit at the end of a bulletin – seemed in danger of taking over factual programming as a whole (see John Langer, *Tabloid Television: Popular Journalism and the 'Other News'*, Routledge, 1998).

THE DOCUMENTARY TRADITION

Is there a way to disentangle documentary from Reality TV, in order to place the latter alongside its entertainment industry counterparts? One route is to analyse Reality TV against the historical backdrop of the documentary tradition. By revisiting some of the debates over documentary ethics and methods that fired up 1960s' practitioners, we can set Reality TV in its historical context. Documentary's claims to provide a 'real' account of the world are bound up with the evolution of the genre itself. Simultaneously, such claims became the proverbial rod for documentary's own back. Any reconstruction, any coaching of interviewees, any dilution of portrayed events for the sake of, say, cinematic conventions or audience expectations: all were hostages to fortune, sticks with which to beat a broad spectrum of filmmakers, from Robert Flaherty to Errol Morris. Depending on an audience's scepticism, documentary's truth-claims can either bolster its reputation or open it up to increased scrutiny. Consider the following analogy: using rules seldom applied to musicals, thrillers are often condemned as unrealistic. So, too, non-fiction film and video: the claim to tell the truth quite rightly invites a degree of examination not seen elsewhere. For those caught faking it, as opposed to *Faking It*, the penalties can be severe, both from the broadcasting authorities and in terms of lost credibility among viewers (and advertisers/ overseas buyers).

No doubt recent scepticism about objective truth impacts upon documentary makers too. It appears that since the 1960s, self-belief has declined, whether by accident or design. Certainly to contemporary audiences, the 'golden age' of US network documentary can seem little more than Cold War propaganda; that which carries an official stamp of approval invites present-day distrust (see Michael Curtin, 'The Discourse of "Scientific Anti-Communism" in the "Golden Age" of Documentary', *Cinema Journal*, vol. 32, no. 1, Fall 1992). Documentary makers ignore a less naïve audience at their peril.

Part of today's loss of nerve is internally generated. Back in the 1960s, the most innovative forms of documentary work eschewed the tone of complete 'expertise' pervading television and avoided claims to have privileged access to the truth. An eminent film historian notes that 'ciné verité's foregoing of "authoritarian" voiceover narration' stems from films where 'no assertions have absolute authority … Truth is to be revealed, not asserted by a narrator whose authority is not to be questioned' (William Rothman, *Documentary Film Classics*, Cambridge University Press, 1997). This indicates that, whilst there was a relativist strand in the most innovative 1960s works, it was nevertheless informed by a desire to investigate, thereby unearthing information and making it available to an audience. Viewers appeared to reciprocate, seeing classic documentary as truthful precisely because of the effort put into obtaining the footage that was subsequently presented to them in a non-judgemental way. Whether or not viewers believed 1960s documentaries is almost irrelevant here; audiences distinguished non-fiction film from other genres. They saw them as distinct from the entertainment elsewhere in the schedules because they appeared to conduct a search for the truth. Contrast this with today's scenario, where reluctance to make claims to knowledge leaves advocates of Reality TV pushing at an open door.

The different mindsets are striking even when considering an old artefact such as a training manual first published in 1963 (W. Hugh Baddeley, *The Technique of Documentary Film Production*, Focal Press, 1975). Addressing budding documentarians, the author offered the following advice on the 'factual or documentary film' ('an instrument with a thousand serious jobs to do'): 'It is called upon to tell us about the world we live in; to present us with its myriad faces; to show us our fellow men spread about the six continents; to show us nature, inanimate and living, in all its moods.' In closing, the author drew to a halt the comprehensive technical advice and paused to praise the 'idealism of the documentary pioneers who had, in fact, some quite mundane subjects to deal with themselves. But they brought them alive. They saw the drama and significance of everyday life and wove them into their films and succeeded in giving their audience a new sense of awareness'. One such documentary pioneer, Paul Rotha, endorsed Baddeley's volume with an enthusiastic introduction.

While novice documentary makers were being advised to combine technical proficiency with a moral mission, those at the head of their profession were discarding this approach. This is best expressed in the division between the makers of US direct cinema and French ciné vérite. Both 'schools' sought to reveal the truth of their particular subject matter whilst rejecting the conventions of the voice-over and the externally imposed narrative interpretation. An unashamedly anthropological methodology would enable a closer understanding of those on camera, both as individuals and as people caught up in impersonal social forces.

There were certainly differences between the two movements. Americans like D.A. Pennebaker and Frederick Wiseman adopted a seemingly neutral and non-interventionist stance, blending in until their protagonists relaxed around them so that the 'real' persona could emerge. Conversely, French filmmakers like Jean Rouch valued transparency at the point of exhibition, where he, his crew and even his equipment was in plain sight, often interrupting participants and demanding more information. Whilst US non-participant observers acted like a 'fly on the wall', their Parisian counterparts declared themselves the flies in the soup. Hence unusual methods: shocking conventional filmmakers with huge shot ratios or ending a piece by showing the subjects a rough cut, filming their responses and editing these into the finished piece. Debate raged over whether to keep a low profile while filming or candidly admit on camera that 'this is a film': what was at issue, on the surface at least, was which of these approaches best captured reality. The goal was to get closer to 'the truth' than the conventional ethnographic film, with its archive footage and sometimes staged scenes, all bound up in an omniscient narration.

Today this controversy represents little more than an historical curiosity. The films survive and *Chronicle of a Summer* (1960), *Primary* (1960), *Don't Look Back* (1966) and *High School* (1968) are all regarded as classics of the genre, irrespective of past labels and polemics. Among contemporary audiences, there is a greater awareness of the ways in which non-fiction film can be contrived. As techniques such as reconstruction become more familiar, viewer scepticism grows accordingly (see Brian Winston, *Claiming the Real*, BFI Publishing, 1995). Media studies textbooks inform undergraduate readers of 'an outburst of criticism, accusing ... early documentary makers of inauthenticity and deception' (Patricia Holland, *The Television Handbook*, Routledge, 2000). Coinciding with such criticism is the way that the techniques associated with both documentary schools have moved from being experimental to being mainstream, leaving the casual observer to wonder what the sharp methodological differences were all about in the first place. Transatlantic rivalries aside, there seems little sense in clinging onto the old categories. As one commentator put it, 'The distinction between "cinéma-vérité" and "direct cinema" is not a viable one' (William Rothman, *Documentary Film Classics*, 1997). Nevertheless, reminded of a time when such distinctions seemed to matter, it is apparent that something serious was at stake back then which is absent from current controversies over Reality TV.

Can such changes be explained in technological terms? In Baddeley's book, technical competence is the main preoccupation and many current documentary opportunities are possible thanks to technological changes. This invites further parallels with the 1960s, when increasingly portable synch sound equipment and the lightweight Éclair camera gave filmmakers increased freedom of movement. There would be no scope to truly accompany John F. Kennedy on the campaign trail without cameras capable of being shoulder-mounted or hand-held. (In later years, video as a cheaper alternative to film stock was also to make an incredible impact.) Without suitable equipment, non-fiction film would have been stuck in the 1940s (although interestingly, the British documentary film movement disdained 16mm film stock, which it saw as intrinsically linked to amateurism; see Brian Winston, *Technologies of Seeing: Photography, Cinematography and Television*, BFI Publishing, 1996). Documentary aesthetics can be the product of technological change – in the style of Errol Morris's 'Interrotron' – but that does not mean that there is a technological explanation of present trends.

First of all, video and especially digital video (DV) allows for cheaper and smaller equipment, bringing the advantages of miniaturization similar to those of the Éclair camera, with the added bonus of facilitating covert surveillance work. Furthermore, champions of DV point to its sharpness and clarity, which they praise as being of broadcast quality and comparable to film. Critics of the format disagree on both counts, but its existence has fuelled the belief that anyone can be in film production, as new technologies slash costs. What is apparently good for the production goose also applies to the post-production gander. Whereas the post-Steenbeck edit suite relied upon expensive equipment such as Avid, new desktop applications can potentially reduce the cost of producing an online edit of a new documentary. Taken together, digital video and non-linear editing represent a considerable reduction of at least the hypothetical costs of documentary production. (These trends are not confined to non-fiction filmmaking, as suggested by the notoriety and appeal of the Dogme 95 manifesto. Each of the 16,000 subscribers to the Shooting People listserv is confronted daily with requests for their unpaid services on no-budget DV features.) Needless to say, this technological scope to cut costs does not necessarily translate into quality programming; at the level of production values, money will out.

Indeed, technologically minded critics of Reality TV point to cheap but high quality videotape as a source of cheap, poor quality programmes. Whereas the sheer cost of filming usually forces all outside Hollywood to 'edit in camera' and be selective about the number of shots used and takes, the comparative cheapness of video allows one to carry on shooting, in the belief that sufficient footage will provide something to put right in post-production. (In the other common form of Reality TV, the video clip show, footage is acquired outright from individuals, authorities or under the auspices of the police (for example, *Cops*), so filmstock versus tape is not an issue). Scope to shoot seemingly unlimited amounts of footage exempts the reality programme maker from some of the potentially disciplinary role of budgeting. It is cheaper to uncover Ibiza if one only has to store tapes at the end of the day, rather than sending the daily rushes off to be developed.

From an historical point of view, purely technical explanations for the paucity of reality programming are wrong. If we consider 1960s' documentary innovation, shockingly high shot ratios (sometimes 20:1) were the norm. After gathering miles of footage and spending months in the edit suite, worthwhile results emerged. Aiming to 'wrap' in a short space of time with maximum cost-cutting was anathema to Wiseman *et al.* (at considerable personal cost, since such methods repelled commercial backers). Instead, belief in the intrinsic value of the subject matter and the potential of the medium to explore it paved the way for an impressive body of work. Content-led, ciné vérité and direct cinema worked around technical barriers far greater than those facing contemporary filmmakers with access to video. One wonders what could have been produced had DV been around 40 years ago.

There is also something Luddite about blaming mini-DV for contemporary laziness and banality. Having both shot in and taught with the format, I would accept that it still struggles to compare favourably with film, even despite the film effects and plug-ins available to non-linear editors. Those mourning the golden age of discipline and 'editing in camera' would do well to recall that all this and more is possible with new video technologies. In fact, you only have to survey the 'making of' extras on a Soderberg or Aronofsky DVD, to see that the best younger filmmakers take planning and pre-production very seriously indeed. When new technology really does make a difference to production – as in *Big Brother*'s live webcam feeds (utterly impossible with film) – the vast majority of content was exceedingly dull. In riposte to the technology fetishists, we should recall that content is king: after all, no station would decline the Rodney King beating tape or the Zapruder footage on 'broadcast quality' grounds.

The preceding historical detour reminds us of a time when filmmakers made an impassioned case for getting closer to the truth and boldly stated the superiority of their methods. The contrast with the present demonstrates how far we have travelled since those heady days: seldom do the methods for creating Reality TV excite any real debate, apart from the odd expression of ethical qualms or technical wonderment. This might appear to be progress: whereas the shining stars of post-war documentary seemed obsessed with form, a combination of videotape and a popular touch allow contemporary audiences to get straight to the heart of reality programmes. Yet the opposite is more accurate – precisely because the content mattered, French and American documentarists took their methodologies seriously. Documentary making *per se* was of little interest to a Rouch or a Pennebaker: what mattered was getting to the core of the subject in order to best represent it. This thoroughness paid off. Rather than deal merely with the particular institutions on camera, *Titicut Follies* and *High School* reputedly allow insight into all mental hospitals and educational establishments respectively. The depth of each specific investigation means the documentary can seem to typify its subject matter.

Effective documentary making was (and is) a serious undertaking. Hours of footage would be edited down to create the final 90-minute or two-hour version. Although today's media-savvy viewers might point to the role of editing in creating the final product and influencing viewers accordingly, 1960s' documentarists tended to be scrupulously fair in giving their subjects enough celluloid rope before splicing together a preferred readings of events. Technological preconditions aside, the will and tenacity involved in recording and representing something suggests a topic worthy of the effort. Hence the discomfort that sometimes underpinned official responses to the documentaries delivering an exposé of injustice or institutional negligence. In other words, the range of human emotions shown in the most powerful documentaries could impact upon policy or institutions, changing reality itself. Both direct cinema and ciné vérité were unashamedly intended to search out 'the truth' and reconstruct it on the screen in the most persuasive way possible. This concern with content roots both movements in the non-fiction film tradition far more than their present-day Reality TV counterparts. A paradox for today is that the idea of objectivity and objective reality is in decline, while support for Reality TV is firmed up by it being seen as 'more real' than its predecessors.

BACK TO REALITY

The growth of reality programming or tabloid television would matter less were it not so central to the non-fiction output of so many broadcasters. Much of this essay has argued that we should disentangle reality programming from documentary, the better to get 'back to reality'. Let's treat the clip shows, docusoaps and 'social experiments' as entertainment and be done with it. Thankfully some broadcasters have made a step in this direction, such as Channel 4's digital offshoot E4, which marketed *Big Brother Live* (the sanitized video feed version) alongside *Banzai* and the *Sopranos*. Let's see a 'non-factual' rebranding of reality shows.

That said, we should consider whether reality programming is even worth using as entertainment. Like most distractions, it can give us something to talk about. As University of Alberta Professor Aniko Bodroghkozy explains, reality shows do what soap operas did in the past by providing a context for people to get together and gossip without offending others: '*Survivor*, like all successful television, is polythematic, an open text that allows different readings. People can use the show as a launching pad to think about and discuss the workplace, capitalism and relationships in 21st century' (Gilbert A. Bouchard, 'The escape to Reality TV', posted at www.expressnews.ualberta.ca). Tellingly, even our banal chit-chat seems tempered by our insecurities over workplace relationships. Yet in the hands of the broadcasters and rating demographers, such talk is reconfigured as the fabled water-cooler moment.

One could speculate at length as to why ordinary seeming individuals (accompanied by the mandatory lap dancer) and situations are such a staple of the entertainment schedules, pushing aside soap operas and those gameshows which are unwilling to introduce a large dollop of 'reality' into proceedings, in the sweaty-browed style of *Who Wants to be a Millionaire?* As several commentators have noted, our collective willingness to watch such material indicates an erosion of the distinction between public and private, an end to intimacy and an entertainment industry prepared to cannibalize personal mishaps in pursuit of ratings. Slovenian philosopher Slavoj Žižek expressed discomfort about where this could all lead, admitting that, despite his decadent tastes, he was shocked by the existence of lavatory webcams (http://www.spiked-online.com/Articles/00000002D2C4.htm). Meanwhile Daniel Minihan's excellent satire *Series 7: The Contenders* (2001) combined *Cops*, *Big Brother* and *Gladiators* to present a fictional gameshow in which contestants have to bump each other off. So ingrained are 'the rules' in the movie that few question how society got to the stage where strangers picked by lottery are given guns and told to cause fatalities to amuse the rest of us. A work of fiction, but unnervingly life-like.

Talk of *Series 7* is a reminder that the rise of Reality TV has a knock-on effect for the fake documentary as a form of fictional narrative. In Britain, Ruggero Deodato's gruesome *Cannibal Holocaust* (1979) was banned for nearly 20 years, partly on account of the conceit of it being 'lost footage'. John McNaughton's *Henry: Portrait of a Serial Killer* (1986) was recut by the censor at the point where bogus camcorder inserts implicated the viewer in Otis and Henry's crimes: its independent, documentary feel meant it was treated more harshly than its mainstream gothic horror counterpart, *Silence of the Lambs* (1990). More recently, *The Blair Witch Project* (1999) prospered, in part thanks to rumours that it was an authentic documentary. Despite today's sceptical attitudes towards any claims to 'represent the real', the continuing appeal of fiction with a documentary look (and the documentary drama genre itself) suggests the evocative power of the phrase 'based on a true story'. We yearn for reality even as we doubt the possibility of ever capturing it on film or tape.

CONCLUSION: BLAME THE AUDIENCE?

Who is this 'we'? In closing, there is one aspect of current criticisms of tabloid TV from which the present essay stands apart. This is the tendency simply to blame the audience for its lack of taste and discernment. Opponents of Reality TV mirror those who champion it. Whereas some praise the genre for its inclusive and democratic character, others complain of 'pandering to the lowest common denominator', a theme expressed by satirists and TV critics alike. No doubt the pursuit of ratings is a factor in the fatuous content we often endure, but this is based as much upon network guesswork as upon what people really want. The spectacular failure of the glossy UK version of *Survivor* is evidence of this.

More seriously, such arguments seriously underestimate the capacity of the audience to reason and work things out for themselves. Whilst formally complaining about the media, pundits often end up venting their spleen against media consumers, particularly the working class (see Andrew Calcutt, 'Democracy Under Threat' in Hugh Stephenson and Michael Bromley (eds), *Sex, Lies and Democracy: The Press and the Public*, Longman, 1998). Take *Jerry Springer* in the late 1990s – it seemed that the lower the researchers trawled for guests to use as freak show exhibits, the higher the ratings would go. Many allegations of fakery and a homicide later, a combination of backlash and ratings slump forced the show to tone it down. Admittedly, such pressures were often informed by snobbery towards Springer's perceived white trash audience, but they undermine the myth of the gormless, compliant viewer, sucking up whatever the broadcasters are prepared to dollop out.

When it comes to factual programming, reality is in the eye of the beholder, although not in the way postmodern 'reader-response criticism' would understand it. We are only formally free to assemble any meaning we like from the free-floating signifiers of a TV text; in practice, we have to work with the material we're given. The classic fly-on-the-wall documentary recognized this; although cleverly selecting and editing from mountains of footage, the filmmakers refused to openly editorialize, leaving us free to draw our own conclusions. This tradition carries on to this day. Thus, whereas at first glance Frederick Wiseman's recent *Domestic Violence* (2001) draws us into 'victim culture' and a dysfunctional, *Springer*-style Florida milieu, its actual meaning remains open to interpretation. The three hours spent with wife-beaters and the police and in a women's refuge is no doubt meant to make us hostile to violent spouses. Yet do we also note the suspension of the presumption 'innocent until proven guilty' for alleged batterers and the therapeutic indoctrination of their victims in the hostel? How might this open up into a critique of institutions?

As discerning viewers we sift through material and make sense of it as we see fit. This capacity alone should inoculate us against the spread of 'reality programming' at the expense of documentary and investigative journalism.

AFTERWORD
Dolan Cummings

'What is truth?' Pontius Pilate asked Christ. Christ didn't answer. After all, it is a very hard question. But anybody who has taken the time to think about it can see that there is a difference between truth and reality. Reality is the way things are; truth is how we make sense of it. We do this by imaginatively reconstructing reality in our own minds. Language and literature allow us to communicate our ideas about the world, however accurate or inaccurate they might be, and so does television.

As the contributors to this book have shown, representing reality on television is no simple matter. The documentary tradition described by Graham Barnfield and Bernard Clark has always been about a struggle to reconstruct situations and events in a coherent and comprehensible way. As with any exercise in truth-telling, there is a subjective element to this. Like any author, a documentary-maker has to interpret for him or herself before he or she can communicate the truth to others. Despite the rhetoric used by some practitioners, documentary has never been about simply pointing a camera. That doesn't mean that documentaries are necessarily fake, but it does mean that they are imperfect. Reality TV does away with pretensions to 'truth', and tends instead to focus on entertainment.

All that said, it should be clear from the essays in this collection that there is more to Reality TV than documentary, 'dumbed down' or otherwise. What all reality programmes share, whether they are documentary or light entertainment, is a belief in connecting directly with the audience and a rejection of old-fashioned hierarchies. While Reality TV tends to be promoted as entertainment, then, it also reflects trends that are affecting not only television, but creative and even scholarly enterprise more broadly.

In particular, many Reality TV programmes seem to share a particular idea of what they mean by 'real'. The focus is very much on individuals rather than institutions, and the aspiration is to achieve psychological insight, rather than to explain their lives. As Victoria Mapplebeck put it in her essay, 'Following the shift from public to private, epitomized by the talk shows, documentaries are almost exclusively about personal rather than public crisis.' The same goes all the more for programmes without documentary pretensions. To this end, participants in Reality TV programmes are often taken out of their normal environments, away from their homes, their families and their jobs, and put in artificial situations. The idea seems to be that when you strip away the trappings of civilization, responsibility and social expectations, you are left with the real person.

This thinking is certainly apparent in *Survivor*, with its primeval overtones. In *Big Brother*, the focus on personality is even stronger because the setting is so banal. The programme has tended to feature long, rambling, fairly childish conversations between housemates lounging around with nothing else to do. Perhaps this aspect of Reality TV has something in common with the strain in psychology that deals with the 'inner child'. Certainly the particular view of reality it expresses is part of a broader social shift towards a psychotherapeutic concern with the self, which is also expressed in the growth of focus groups and emotionalism more generally.

While this sort of thing has had a certain amount of appeal as TV, it seems that producers are keen to stir things up a little. As both Bernard Clark and Christopher Dunkley have noted in their essays, Reality TV is taking on an increasingly nasty aspect. US audiences have been shocked by programmes such as *The Chair* and *The Chamber*, in which participants have been gently tortured, and there is speculation that something similar is bound to appear sooner or later on British TV. Already, Sky One has broadcast *Fear Factor*, whose participants face their greatest fears (snakes, rats, heights) for cash prizes. *Big Brother* itself is spicing up the tasks required of contestants by offering more extreme rewards and forfeits. Is Reality TV spiralling into decline?

It has been argued that Reality TV is a flash in the pan and that it has no future. Even disregarding what Christopher Dunkley calls 'Humiliation TV' though, there are indications that the phenomenon is here to stay. At the time of writing, there are a number of new Reality TV shows being talked about. In the BBC's *Diners*, a variety of guests – some celebrities, some ordinaries – are filmed over dinner in a specially designed restaurant, with the cameras hopping from table to table depending on where the most interesting (or irresistibly banal) conversation is taking place. Meanwhile, Endemol, the company behind *Big Brother*, is working on *The People's Club*, which will allow viewers to make management decisions for a league football club. The focus on 'ordinary people', both as subjects and as interacting viewers, is more enduring than any particular format.

This development can be looked at in a number of ways. It can be seen as 'democratization'. The shift from authoritarian broadcasters making programmes about 'important' people and subjects, to interactive television companies involving viewers in programmes about 'ordinary Joes', is certainly an important one. On one hand it perhaps reflects the breakdown of old-fashioned prejudices and elitism. On the other, it can be seen as a crisis of standards, or a loss of nerve on the part of broadcasters. This is closely related to the argument about 'dumbing down'. How you feel about that debate is likely to influence your thoughts about the merits of Reality TV. Nonetheless, it is quite possible to enjoy *Big Brother* while lamenting the demise of more serious programmes.

There are still plenty of highbrow programmes available, but many of these seem to share some of Reality TV's assumptions about the need to connect with audiences in more direct and accessible ways. Have current affairs programmes and dramas, for example, undergone a similar transformation? Does television about 'ordinary people' tell us something about ourselves, or does it simply create disposable celebrities for our entertainment? Does the focus on personality mean that television is losing the ability to tell us about the bigger picture and to put things in context? Finally, is it possible to object to such developments without endorsing the elitism and hierarchies of the past? The contributors to this collection have given us their ideas: it is up to the reader to decide how true, or how real, those ideas are.

DEBATING MATTERS

Institute of Ideas
Expanding the Boundaries of Public Debate

If you have found this book interesting,
and agree that 'debating matters', you can
find out more about the Institute of Ideas
and our programme of live conferences and
debates by visiting our website
www.instituteofideas.com.
Alternatively you can email
info@instituteofideas.com
or call 020 7269 9220 to receive a full
programme of events and information about
joining the Institute of Ideas.

Other titles available in this series:

DEBATING MATTERS

Institute of Ideas
Expanding the Boundaries of Public Debate

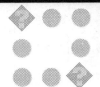

ETHICAL TOURISM:

WHO BENEFITS?

The idea of 'responsible tourism' has grown in popularity over the past decade. But who benefits from this notion? Should the behaviour of travellers come under scrutiny? What are the consequences of this new etiquette for the travelling experience? Can we make a positive difference if we change the way the travel?

Contrasting responses to these questions come from:

- Dea Birkett, columnist for *The Guardian* and author of *Amazonian*
- Jim Butcher, Senior Lecturer, Department of Geography and Tourism, Canterbury Christ Church University College
- Paul Goldstein, Marketing Manager, Exodus Travel
- Dr Harold Goodwin, Director of the Centre for Responsible Tourism at the University of Greenwich
- Kirk Leech, Assistant Director of the youth charity Worldwrite

ANIMAL EXPERIMENTATION:

GOOD OR BAD?

Some argue that animal experiments are vital to advance scientific knowledge and improve medical practice. Others believe that they are unnecessary, cruel and repetitive. Do animals experience pain and suffering in the same ways as humans; if so should they be given rights? Is a compromise between animal rights campaigners and those who emphasize the needs of humans possible or even desirable?

Key figures in the debate exchange their views on this contentious issue:

- Dr Stuart Derbyshire, scientist at the University of Pittsburgh, US, researching central mechanisms of pain
- Dr Mark Matfield, medical research scientist
- Dr Tom Regan, Professor of Philosophy and President of The Culture & Animals Foundation
- Dr Richard D. Ryder, author of *Painism: a Modern Morality*.

ABORTION:

WHOSE RIGHT?

Currently around 180 000 British women terminate pregnancies each year – far more than the politicians who passed the Abortion Act in 1967 intended. Should the law be made more liberal to reflect demand for abortion? Is the problem that in Britain, women still do not have the 'right to choose'? Or is it too easy for women to 'take the life' of their 'unborn children'? What role should doctors play in the abortion decision?

Contrasting answers are presented in this book by:

- Ann Furedi, director of communications, British Pregnancy Advisory Service
- Mary Kenny, journalist and writer
- Theodore Darymple, GP and author of *Mass Listeria: The Meaning of Health Scares* and *An Intelligent Person's Guide to Medicine.*
- Emily Jackson, Lecturer in Law, London School of Economics
- Helen Watt, director, Linacre Centre for Healthcare Ethics.

ART:

WHAT IS IT GOOD FOR?

Art seems to be more popular and fashionable today than ever before. At the same time, art is changing, and much contemporary work does not fit into the categories of the past. Is 'conceptual' work art at all? Should artists learn a traditional craft before their work is considered valuable? Can we learn to love art, or must we take it or leave it?

These questions and more are discussed by:

- David Lee, art critic and editor of *The Jackdaw*
- Ricardo P. Floodsky, editor of artrumour.com
- Andrew McIlroy, an international advisor on cultural policy
- Sacha Craddock, an art teacher and critic
- Pavel Buchler, Professor of Art and Design at Manchester Metropolitan University
- Aidan Campbell, art critic and author.

THE INTERNET:

BRAVE NEW WORLD?

Over the last decade, the internet has become part of everyday life. Along with the benefits however, come fears of unbridled hate speech and pornography. More profoundly, perhaps, there is a worry that virtual relationships will replace the real thing, creating a sterile, soulless society. How much is the internet changing the world?

Contrasting answers come from:

- Peter Watts, lecturer in Applied Social Sciences at Canterbury Christ Church University College
- Chris Evans, lecturer in Multimedia Computing and the founder of Internet Freedom
- Ruth Dixon, Deputy Chief Executive of the Internet Watch Foundation
- Helene Guldberg and Sandy Starr, Managing Editor and Press Officer respectively at the online publication *spiked*.

DESIGNER BABIES:

WHERE SHOULD WE DRAW THE LINE?

Science fiction has been preoccupied with technologies to control the characteristics of our children since the publication of Aldous Huxley's *Brave New World*. Current arguments about 'designer babies' almost always demand that lines should be drawn and regulations tightened. But where should regulation stop and patient choice in the use of reproductive technology begin?

The following contributors set out their arguments:

- Juliet Tizzard, advocate for advances in reproductive medicine
- Professor John Harris, ethicist
- Veronica English and Ann Sommerville of the British Medical Association
- Josephine Quintavalle, pro-life spokesperson
- Agnes Fletcher, disability rights campaigner.